Laying the Elegant Table

Laying the Elgant Table

China, Faience, Porcelain, Majolica,
Glassware, Flatware, Tureens, Platters,
Trays, Centerpieces, Tea Sets

BY

INÈS HEUGEL

PHOTOGRAPHS BY

CHRISTIAN SARRAMON

Rizzoli NEW YORK

CONTENTS

Title page:
A dresser mellowed by time, a quilted
tablecloth, fine earthenware, and
delicate porcelain bought over the years
from secondhand dealers and shops:
these are some of the pleasures in store
for anyone with more than a passing
interest in the art of the table.

Preceding pages:

Detail of *The Wedding Meal at Yport*,
oil on canvas by Albert Fourie, 1886.
Musée de Rouen.

Opposite:

The display of a passionate collector:
Limoges porcelain cake and dessert
service (1860); English tea set (1910);
bone china tea and coffee set (1910).

The Art of Table Setting

From the spartan boards of the Middle Ages to the tables of our grandmothers, the laying of tables has evolved in step with technical advances in the manufacture of china, earthenware, glass, and metals. At the same time, it has been heavily influenced by the structure and organization of society.

A pretty tablecloth and fine English tableware for an *al fresco* meal.

Tankards and Trenchers

In medieval Europe, there was no such thing as a dining room. Instead, a long, narrow trestle table was set up in any room of the house that happened to suit the occasion. The diners sat elbow to elbow, on only one side of the board. A simple white linen cloth was spread, folded double on the diners' side of the table so they could use the slack to wipe their hands and mouths. The shared double-folded table napkin was eventually abandoned in favor of the towel, a separate piece of fabric laid on the main cloth. A trencher made of wood or metal served as a plate, along with a piece of bread on which successive foods were served. The diners ate with their fingers and left their sauce-soaked bread to be shared among the servants after the main meal. Sometimes, in order to reduce the workload for the servants, a flat-bottomed tin porringer with handles or lugs on either side might be placed between two guests. Using big spoons, which would be vermeil-plated in rich men's houses and in poorer establishments were made of pewter or wood, the various meats would be served in these bowls along with their sauces. The fork had not yet been invented, and pointed table knives, which began to appear at the table in the fourteenth and fifteenth centuries, were used to spear food and carry it to the mouth. Wine, often diluted with water, was served in a shared tankard, with guests taking turns to drink from it.

The Coming of the Fork

From the sixteenth century onward, the tablecloth was still white, either made of linen or cotton, and with damask religious or military motifs. It was laid on the table with its ironed pleats fully apparent, accompanied by ample, skillfully folded individual napkins. As the decades went on, napkin folds became more and more elaborate and sophisticated, taking the shapes of birds, butterflies, trees, flowers, seashells, and fish. The men knotted them around their necks to protect their fashionable but voluminous lace collars. The fork, which had come into use in Italy in the fifteenth century, was introduced to France by Catherine de Médicis at the court of her son Henri III. In its early stages, the fork had only two teeth and was used by several people at a sitting; for this reason it was viewed as unhygienic and took a while to catch on.

1.

Individual Place Settings

By the seventeenth century, people carried their own knives and forks in a case attached to their belt. The handles of the knife and fork varied in color according to the church calendar: white at Easter, black during Lent, and black and white at Pentecost. The host provided each guest with his own pewter plate and sometimes a goblet. Various prominent figures made contributions to the arts of the table—notably Cardinal Mazarin, who invented the concave plate (known as the *assiette à la cardinale*), and Richelieu, who brought round-bladed table knives into fashion. By the end of the century, matching forks and spoons were routinely placed next to plates at meals, while flowers made their appearance in the middle of the table, side by side with the vessels containing salt and spices.

The Sumptuous Tables of the Eighteenth Century

In the eighteenth century, meals all over Europe were predominantly served in the French style. Everything would be prepared before the guests' arrival, and tables were magnificently set. The plates were of fine china or soft-paste porcelain from a leading pottery, and the utensils were made of silver or vermeil. Knives, forks, and spoons were placed in such a way as to show off the armorial bearings engraved on them. The dishes for the first course would be served according to a precise and practiced order, with dish-covers to keep the food hot. As soon as all the guests were seated, the servants uncovered all the dishes at the same time, to dramatic effect. After the guests had eaten as much as they wanted of the first course, a second set of utensils was laid, then a third, and so on. The middle of the table was dominated by a centerpiece of silver or porcelain, which contained spices and served as a base for lamps and candles. Only one glass was provided per person, and each glass was placed in a basin of ice on a sideboard or dresser big enough to contain one or several glasses at a time. In the latter case, its rim would be notched so the glasses could be sloped into molds within the ice. Meanwhile the wine bottles were placed in other basins or coolers. From 1750 and onward, damask tablecloths gave way to white-on-white embroidered tablecloths.

The Russian Style

In the nineteenth century, houses began to be structured in a different way. In general their rooms were smaller, and one room was definitively set aside for dining. The arrival of vast quantities of imported Indian cotton in England created a revolution of sorts; cotton replaced the old table linen, which was now enriched with open-work, embroidery, or appliqué. At the same time, the napkin grew more discreet, and its folding became a much simpler affair. The French style of serving meals

1.

2.

3.

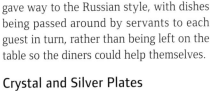

gave way to the Russian style, with dishes being passed around by servants to each guest in turn, rather than being left on the table so the diners could help themselves.

Crystal and Silver Plates

The first major breakthrough in table setting was the arrival of crystal in France in the late eighteenth century, after its invention a century earlier by the English craftsman Ravenscroft. This led to the appearance of individual glasses—between three and six—on the table, for each different drink served. The second novelty was the invention by another Englishman, Elkington, of a silver plating process, which was immediately taken up in France by Christofle. This period also saw the beginnings of industrially produced knives, forks, and spoons, which allowed the new middle classes to match the aristocracy when it came to entertaining, at considerably lesser expense. Toward the end of the nineteenth century, specially shaped pieces began to gain importance: new items appeared for the table—such as fish knives and forks, oyster forks, sugar tongs, and dishes and plates specifically designed for asparagus, artichokes, or shellfish—while accessories, such as knife

rests and napkin rings, were invented in response to the dining habits of a brand new middle class. Tablecloths generally stayed white, though colored embroideries were no longer the exception.

The Modern Table

In its time, art nouveau imposed its gentle shapes and undulating lines on the table, as it did on everything else. Tablecloths at the turn of the nineteenth century were more elaborate, being finely stitched with openwork, lace, and tone-on-tone embroidered flowers and insects. Knives, forks, and spoons bore exuberant vegetable motifs while larger pieces of tableware, though still busy in their effect, lost much of their late-nineteenth-century heaviness and pomposity. In the 1920s, the tablecloth finally became an object entirely of color, though its timid pastel tones were sometimes blended with white. At the same time, it became lighter and lighter, and was sometimes replaced by place mats. Organdy and cotton tablecloths with matching napkins—ever smaller in size—were all the rage: and before long cutlery was also redesigned for greater simplicity, acquiring colors of its own in the form of shagreen or semi-precious stone handles.

5.

7.

DINNERWARE

Old porcelain and earthenware plates have survived until today
in every conceivable shape, color, and design and decorated
with flowers, Asian motifs, animals, figures, and landscapes.
Many are still being reproduced. We love them for their beauty,
for the traditional skills, and talents they express, but also for
what they evoke: Sunday lunches at a grandmother's house, for
instance, or holidays at a family home. Whereas in the past, a
household possessed one or several complete sets of table
service, each of which included dozens of pieces, today we
tend to buy in smaller batches—for example, six barbotine
dessert plates, a plump vegetable dish, or even a series of
nonmatching plates that share a common color or motif. A
refined table tends to be second degree, exhibiting a mixture of
styles and epochs, and as such is playful and easy to manage.
An immense variety of table services are on offer at flea
markets and antique shops. The opportunity is boundless for
anyone looking to start a personal collection or for those who
simply delight in tables set with an eye for fantasy and fun.

Faience and Porcelain

Fine porcelain or bone china? Printed or painted decoration? In the broad and infinitely varied realm of ceramic terminology, it is not always easy to find your way. Here is a rough summary of what you need to know.

Origins

The first potters took clay and baked it to make it hard. Then, since their terra-cotta was porous, they had the idea of making it waterproof by covering it with varnish or enamel and firing it a second time. Chinese potters were already making ceramics in this method during the Neolithic age. Later, under the Tang dynasty (AD 618–907), merchants began distributing Chinese pottery in as far as the Islamic countries, where the products were immediately copied. During the thirteenth-century Islamic expansion, the new ceramic techniques spread to Europe, notably to Spain and Mallorca. During the Renaissance, the Italians in turn discovered the Hispano-Moresque *majolica* and developed their own techniques for manufacturing it in centers such as Deruta, Urbino, Gubbio, Siena, and Faenza. The French word *faïence* derives from Faenza: emigrant Italians from that town introduced this type of earthenware to France in the sixteenth century. Still, the most significant advance made by European potters was their discovery of the secret of how to make Chinese porcelain— nearly five hundred years after they first became aware of its existence.

Faience Earthenware

Faience, for the French, is pottery made from clay, colored in mass, permeable to water, and loose-textured, which is then covered in an opaque enamel made of a lead-alkaline solution to which tin oxide has been added. This glaze, which hides the original earth tint, can serve as a support for colored design, mainly cobalt blue.

For four centuries after the faience technique arrived in France, potters steadily improved the quality of their pieces. In doing so, they strove to refine their clay mixtures to make them harder and whiter, while at the same time perfecting their decorations using varied colors and ever more elaborate designs.

The first French faience potters in the sixteenth century practiced the technique of *grand feu* (hot firing), meaning they painted their designs directly on the raw enamel, later applying a cover and firing it at a very high temperature. This was the technique used in the great centers of Nevers, Rouen, Moustiers, Strasbourg, and Marseilles, making the best of a process that was unable to fix certain colors, notably reds. However, at the end of the seventeenth century, Hannong of Strasbourg invented *petit feu* (slow firing) procedure, which consisted of applying a polychrome design to a piece that had already been enameled and fired and refiring the piece in a kiln set to a lower temperature. This technique made it possible to fix very fine designs and a range of colors that would not tolerate higher temperatures, such as bright yellow and purple.

2.

3.

4.

Preceding pages:
Plates can be decorated in several ways: by freehand; by a dotted ("pounced") pattern that the painter connects with his brush; by printing; or (as in this case) by stencilling.

1. *Rayonnant* pattern. Manufacture de Rouen, 17th century.

2. Hot-fired faience plate with hunting motif. Manufacture de Moustiers, circa 1740.

3. Hot-fired Italianate faience plate, "Rape of Europe motif," after Francois Chauveau. Manufacture de Nevers, circa 1680.

4. Faience plate, blue monochrome pastoral scene. Manufacture de Nevers, second half of the 17th century.

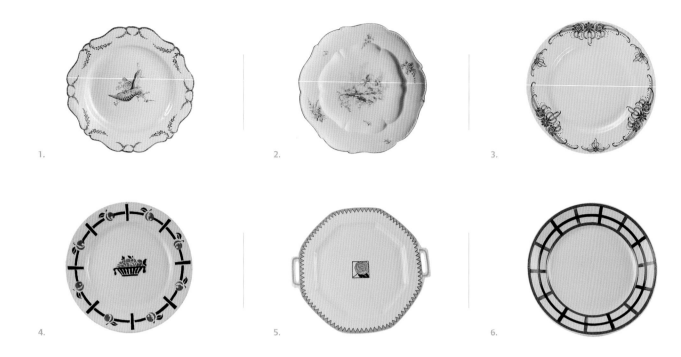

Fine Stoneware

As decorations grew more elaborate, English potters perfected the technique for making what is known as stoneware. Invented in 1720 in Staffordshire, this process was refined by Josiah Wedgwood in 1760. Wedgwood's stoneware was opaque, white or ivory in color, with a fine, dense, and ringing texture; it was also covered in a transparent glaze, relatively hard and consisting of a lead-alkaline mix. Stoneware was fired at a temperature of about 2000°F. The great advances here were in the color of the paste, which was much whiter, with an ever finer texture and much greater strength and durability than before.

The French reacted to the invasion of English stoneware by creating their own stoneware with the help of English potters who had immigrated to France. Throughout the nineteenth century, their pastes continued to improve: beginning with pipe clay, they moved on to the slightly superior Lorraine clay, then to fine stoneware in the English manner, and finally to feldspathic stoneware.

Bone China

Meanwhile, potters continued to pursue the secret of Chinese porcelain manufacture. The first Frenchman to discover a paste approximating to that of the Chinese in 1673 was Edmé Poterat of Rouen. But it was the factory at Saint-Cloud, protected by the King's brother Philippe d'Orléans and later by his son the regent, that perfected this so-called soft-paste porcelain, otherwise known as bone china. Other potteries followed suit, also with the support of illustrious protectors: Chantilly was sponsored by the prince of Condé, Mennecy by the duke of Villeroy, Sceaux by the duchess of Maine, and Vincennes—which later became the *Manufacture Royale de Sèvres*—by the King himself. The privileges they enjoyed allowed these potteries to function without having to worry about competitors and in the certainty that there would be financial support for their research. Throughout the eighteenth century, they continued to produce china of incomparable delicacy. Their privileges, however, were abolished by the Revolution.

1.

2.

3.

1. Faience vegetable dish, with cover and snake-motif knob and handles. Manufacture de Rouen, 18th century.

2. Rococo slow-fired faience compote. Manufacture de Strasbourg, circa 1755.

3. Rocaille porcelain bowl. Manufacture de Chantilly, 18th century.

4 and 5. Studies of shapes and decorations by Félix Bracquemond for a table service and various other objects commissioned by the Haviland porcelain works, circa 1876.

Hard-paste Porcelain

In 1789, a chemist named Boettger, working for a porcelain works at Meissen in Saxony, discovered a deposit of kaolin, the matter of which Chinese porcelain is partly composed, and finally realized the dream of European potters for centuries past: the creation of porcelain as beautiful as that of the Chinese. Boettger's hard-paste porcelain was made from a blend of kaolin, feldspath, and quartz.

The porcelain works of Strasbourg and Niderviller were the first in France to manufacture hard-paste porcelain, using kaolin imported from Saxony. Later, in 1768, a deposit of kaolin was found at Saint-Yrieix, near Limoges, by Mme. Darnet, the wife of a local surgeon, and thereafter hard-paste porcelain production developed in France on a major scale. Sèvres immediately built its own factory in Limoges. In Paris between 1780 and 1840, there were at least fifteen potteries producing porcelain of this type, with its signature whiteness and purity. Before long Limoges had become famous in both Europe and America as a center for porcelain manufacture.

Evolving Styles

In the seventeenth and early eighteenth centuries, faience plates imitated the forms developed by goldsmiths and silversmiths, especially their rocaille lines. They were cut in curved shapes and endowed with rice-grain decorations or ribbed and hand-painted with flowers, Chinese motifs, and foliated scrolls.

Under the Empire, these forms became more severe. Antiquity became the fashion. Plates were often octagonal, with gadroons or Greek borders in relief. Acanthus leaves, oak leaves, and swans were the principal themes of their decoration, invariably applied in a carefully balanced manner.

The Restoration and the July Monarchy in France saw a return to neo-Gothic motifs, and it was followed by a mix of styles known as eclecticism during the reign of Napoleon III, much given to pastiches of the past.

At the end of the nineteenth century, graceful birds or flowers in soft colors were distributed asymmetrically all over plates and dishes: this was the era when all things Japanese were in vogue.

In the early twentieth century, with the appearance of art nouveau, motifs borrowed from nature began to be more stylized. Later, in the 1920s and 1930s, art deco went in the opposite direction, favoring starkness, geometric motifs, and right angles.

TIPS FOR COLLECTORS

Distinguishing faience from porcelain

First, by its appearance: faience is matte and opaque; porcelain is thin and translucent. Second, by its feel: faience will be slightly irregular to the touch, whereas porcelain is regular and its enameling is uniform. Third, by its ring: faience makes a dull noise, but the sound of porcelain is crystalline. The sonority of a piece of porcelain will also reveal its condition—when perfect, its sound is clear and true; when restored, it rings more dully.

Distinguishing hard-paste porcelain from soft-paste boneware

If the dish has a smooth, cold, shiny, and clear-cut—almost sharp—edge, it is probably hard-paste porcelain. Boneware tends to be milkier, warmer, and more fragile.

Gray, pink, or red?

French faience earthenware from the eighteenth century has a bluish glaze. When the plate is turned over, you can see the initial color of the paste used, which in turn will indicate its provenance: the grayer pastes are from northern France, a pink tinge indicates Rouen, and the red is from the south of France.

The secret of the "ladybird"

Hot or slow firing? On the bottom of the plate, look for traces of "ladybirds," **pernettes** in French, which were the tiny dots of clay used by potters to stack the pieces in order to prevent spoiling them by contact with each other. Hot-fired pieces show three ladybird points, while slow-fired pieces show six or nine.

4.

5.

1.

SERVICE NAPLES

CREIL
ET
MONTEREAU

LABRADOR

EMAIL SANS PLOMB
DÉPOSÉ

2.

K
NOTRE-DE
G

LUNÉVILLE·BADONVILLER
·FRANCE·

3.

4.

1. Regional spoon rack with spoons and 18th-century faience dishes.

2. Mark of the *Naples* service. Manufacture de Faience de Creil et Montereau.

3. Mark of the Manufacture de Faïences de Lunéville.

4. A collection of flower-patterned plates in a rustic sideboard.

5. Three Sarreguemines marks: *Tokio*, circa 1900; *Plumes de paon*, July 21, 1875; and *Marguerite*, a mark mentioned in the company's 1900 and 1925 catalogues.

5.

Marks and Signatures

Signatures may consist of the symbol of the factory, its initials, the initials of a craftsman, or the full name of the factory. The older insignia were usually those of the factory's sponsor; for example, Sèvres put the two interlacing L's of Louis XV, and Chantilly sported the Condé hunting horn. Sometimes, notably at Sèvres and Vincennes, the throwers and molders would work in their own small, distinctive signs, which are vital for recognizing certain porcelain pieces that carry no other stamp. After 1753, a letter corresponding to the year of manufacture was added to the usual signatures: A for 1753, B for 1754, and C for 1755. At the end of the alphabet, the next series began with AA, and so on. This dating system did not survive the Revolution.

As a rule, hard-paste porcelain is signed. For those looking for precise identifications, there are manuals that list all known signatures and stamps.

Diameters

In Europe, the classic dinner plate measures between 9 and $9^3/_4$ inches in diameter, while the American plate is broader, at 10 to 11 inches. The presentation plate is a recent invention, deriving from the hotel trade; 11 inches in diameter, its function is largely decorative. When setting tables, it is best to leave at least 16 inches between each plate. The bread-and-butter plate (6 inches), an English invention, goes on the upper left side of the dinner plate, while the crescent salad plate, which eliminates the need to change the main plate, is practical but seldom used. Dessert plates are readied in advance, to be brought in at the right moment.

Dinnerware

Dinnerware as we know them today first appeared during the nineteenth century, with the rise of an upper middle class from the new industrial milieus and the emergence of a bourgeoisie anxious to emulate the powerful. The porcelain and faience industries of the time had developed elaborate techniques to respond to these new demands, producing their wares in reasonably priced series. The house, and more specifically the table, became a way of displaying one's social position. Young brides had their trousseaus, bridegrooms their porcelain and faience. Complete set of dinnerware might run from dozens to literally hundreds of pieces. Essentially they consisted of main dinner plates, soup plates, and dessert plates, along with assorted vegetable dishes, tureens, and bowls.

1.

TAKING CARE OF FINE PORCELAIN AND FAIENCE

To clean off grease marks

Soak the dishes in hot water with organic soap for twenty minutes, then remove stains with a brush. Rinse in cold water, dry, then place in an oven at low temperature (200°F) for half an hour. For persistent marks, repeat the process.

To remove stains

Rinse the piece in fresh water, then apply to the stain a mixture of distilled water (one part) and tap water (three parts), adding a few drops of diluted ammonia (be sure to do this in a well-ventilated area). Then place the piece in a plastic bag for twenty minutes before rinsing in fresh water.

To repair a crack

Clean the crack with a Q-tip and soapy water without submerging the plate. If this is not sufficient to clean it, rub with a toothbrush dipped in a diluted solution of acetone or cellulose. Rinse and dry.

Then, using a toothpick, carefully apply epoxy glue all along the crack. Place the piece in the oven, set at 200°F, for five minutes. This will make the crack open wide enough to draw in the glue.

Remove the plate from the oven, clean off the excess glue with burning alcohol, and apply adhesive tape around the piece. Place back in the oven for ten more minutes and set aside to cool.

1. Examples of different decorations for porcelain dishes. These decorations are sometimes applied around the rim of the plate only, sometimes also on the well.

2. Stylized porcelain service. Manufacture de Creil et Montereau, early 20th century.

Blue and White

Blue and white dinnerware and dishes are very common in every style and decoration and from every period. There is a simple reason for this: cobalt blue is the most amenable pigment in the world and also the most reliable, standing up extraordinarily well to oven heat. Over the centuries, every time a new technique came to light, it was always tested first with blue against a white background. So the family of blue and white ceramics is large and confusing and one in which everyone—the Chinese, the Dutch, the English, and the French—has copied and influenced everyone else. Here are the most important things to know.

2.

3.

The Miracle of Chinese Porcelain

The first reference to blue and white ceramic that comes to mind is Chinese porcelain. In 1295, when Marco Polo returned from his travels in the East, he brought with him a variety of crockery made of material so transparent and white that he baptized it *porcella*, the name of a shellfish resembling it (a less poetic detail is that the shellfish itself was named for its likeness to a sow's vulva).

For several centuries, European potters and alchemists searched incessantly for the secret of this mysterious Chinese material; and indeed it was not until the late sixteenth century that Chinese porcelain began to reach Europe in significant quantities. In 1497, Vasco da Gama rounded the Cape of Good Hope, opening up vast new trading possibilities with the East. The Portuguese were followed by the Dutch, the English, and the French, all of whom had a period when they monopolized this trade. Hundreds of ships began sailing to and fro between the East and the West, loaded with spices and silks and ballasted by the porcelain packed in their holds. Between the early seventeenth and the end of the nineteenth century, millions of pieces, mostly blue and white, were imported into Europe, and the European imitations swelled the influx for two centuries.

Beautiful Blues

Porcelain had been manufactured in China since the Tang dynasty (AD 618–907). It owed its transparency to the composition of its paste—which is a blend of kaolin from Gaoling, a region of China in the province of Jingdezhen, and petuntse, a crystalline rock that was used for the glaze, fired at a temperature of between 2400 and 2650°F. At that temperature, only cobalt blue was entirely reliable.

Under the Ming dynasty (1368–1644), the porcelain industry was mostly concentrated in the same province of Jingdezhen, where, if we are to believe the Jesuit d'Entrecolles, no fewer than three thousand kilns were kept permanently lit. The traditional elements of Chinese design were pagodas, animals (dragons or storks), and flowers (peonies, lotuses, and chrysanthemums).

The first Chinese porcelain made for the foreign market was what the Dutch called *kraak porcelain*, which was blue and white. The center of the dish or plate was occupied by a motif such as a bird, while the edge was divided into eight or twelve compartments, narrow and broad by

4.

1. Blue monochrome decoration of roses on oval dish, late 19th century.

2. Faience dish with Bérain-style decoration. Manufacture de Moustiers, 17th century.

3. *Copenhagen* pattern. Manufacture de Sarreguemines.

4. Faience plate called *Persée délivrant Andromède*. Manufacture de Moustiers, 17th century.

1.

2.

3.

1. *Orphée* bone china, printed plate. Manufacture Utzschneider, Sarreguemines, circa 1900.

2. *Flora* faience plate. Manufacture de Creil et Montereau.

3. Savona dish, Asian-inspired decoration. Manufacture de Nevers, early 17th century.

4. Detail of the rim of a faience plate decorated with a garland in relief.

5. Different tones of blue on 19th- and 20th-century plates.

6. Soft-paste porcelain plate with *à la brindille* decoration. Manufacture de Chantilly, 18th century.

7. Plate with rich floral decoration, late 19th century.

turns, and each contained decorative representations of animals, flowers, and Buddhist symbols.

In the seventeenth century, European aristocrats would commission magnificent services bearing their coats of arms along with nature scenes and landscapes. The fashion for this grew markedly after Louis XIV issued summary decrees directing that all objects in gold and silver had to be melted down to pay for his wars. Little by little, the Chinese themselves began to manufacture objects exclusively destined for Western consumption. During the first two hundred years of the Qing Dynasty (1644–1911), Chinese porcelain manufacturers continued to produce magnificent pieces, but in the nineteenth century their quality dipped, the market was flooded, imitations abounded, and prices fell.

Fine Delft

Having failed for the moment to penetrate the secret of Chinese porcelain, European potters contented themselves with imitating the way it looked. In the early seventeenth century, potters in Delft, Holland, began producing a fine tin-bearing earthenware, hot fired with delicate Chinese motifs, which were carefully reproduced at first and later freely interpreted. Even though the result was neither as solid nor as transparent as Chinese porcelain, the forty-odd Delft factories formed the principal European center for the production of ceramics between 1650 and 1750, and became the champions of a blue and white that was itself copied over and over.

The lambrequins of Rouen

Independently from the popularity of Chinese porcelain, the French were creating blue on white patterns of their own, some of which have survived to this day. Tin-slip (stanniferous) earthenware began to be popular with the French public from the end of the sixteenth century, largely thanks to Masseot Abaquesne who, in 1530, founded a factory in Rouen that began by imitating the then-fashionable Italian style. Later, by the end of the sev-

enteenth century, Rouen invented the blue design known in the nineteenth century as "lambrequin." This was inspired by the edges of the fabrics used by the upholsterers during this period to decorate the drapes and overhead linings of four poster beds. When applied to dishes and plates, this made for a symmetrical decoration of concentric embroidered friezes, which overflowed from the edge into the hollow of the piece. This pattern was later taken up by many of the other French potteries, notably Quimper and Gien.

The Bérain Style

Another world famous pattern was the *Bérain* style. In 1680, Pierre Clérissy founded a faience works at Moustiers, a small village in Haute-Provence. His first patterns were also in different shades of blue and were inspired by the hunting scenes of Antonio Tempesta, a sixteenth-century Florentine painter and engraver; he later moved on to the ornamental motifs of Jean Bérain (1639–1711), the King's designer and the official decorator for the royal galas. Bérain compiled a book of decoration that was enormously and steadily successful for two hundred years. His designs for porcelain were extraordinarily refined; drawing their inspiration from Italian grotesques, they featured small figures, mythical animals, masks, and flowers linked together by garlands, wreaths, and arabesques. Like the lambrequin motifs, these designs remain great classics of French ceramic art, and throughout the eighteenth and nineteenth centuries, they were steadily reproduced by France's manufacturers, especially those in the south.

The Chantilly Brindille

The earthenware manufacturers of the late seventeenth century, in their restless search for the secrets of Chinese porcelain, discovered a soft, creamy paste that allowed the application of very delicate patterns. This paste, having been invented at Rouen, was subsequently developed at

4.

5.

6.

7.

1.

1. Simple Vichy-checked everyday dinnerware, circa 1950.

2, 3, and 4. English earthenware, early 19th century. Each plate has a different bird motif.

Saint-Cloud, Chantilly, and Vincennes (which became Sèvres). Saint-Cloud in particular excelled at lambrequins and *Bérain* blue and white patterns. Chantilly then invented new blue and white designs of its own, which were both discreet and delicate: these were known as *à la brindille* (sprig), *à l'oeuillet bleu* (blue carnation), and *jet d'eau* (fountain) and were successfully copied by Arras.

English Willow Pattern

This hugely popular Chinese-influenced ware, with its weeping willow, was developed in England in the late eighteenth century, probably by Thomas Minton. Minton was then an apprentice engraver, but went on to found the famous factory that bore his name. Willow-pattern china was produced on an industrial scale throughout the nineteenth century. Its basic elements were the willows, but it also featured teahouses, boats, fences, three figures (as a rule), islands, and pairs of birds signifying love. This pattern, much beloved by the English, crossed the Channel and was reproduced in France in northern factories, such as Lille, Calais, and Douai, and in the east of the country. Its production has continued right up to the present day.

Impressions in Blue

In the second half of the nineteenth century and the early twentieth century, most potteries produced ordinary low-priced dinnerware, most of them in a palette of blues. These were sold all over France by peddlers who transported them on donkeys and mules. This was the case of two small communes of the Drôme, Saint-Uze and Saint-Vallien, which produced very hard-wearing faience, similar to stoneware and decorated with simple blue flowers. Along with such ordinary services, better quality ones with more elegant patterns were produced for the middle class. At last the latter was able to buy themselves complete services, run-

ning into the hundreds of pieces, which now hit the market in huge quantity. Now they could entertain like the aristocracy and the *grande bourgeoisie*. Not only the faience potteries, but also the porcelain factories depended largely on sales of such services in the second half of the nineteenth century and the early twentieth, shifting with the trend from art nouveau patterns to the more geometric outlines of art deco. This was the case of Creil, Montereau, Sarreguemines, and above all Gien. Founded in 1823, the Gien factory quickly began specializing in personalized, often numbered services. At the same time, it supplied perfect imitations of all the older styles, and after 1860 reverted to blue and white reprises of Rouen and Moustiers.

TIPS FOR COLLECTORS

Blue and white earthenware and porcelain have always been collectible.

Louis XIV and many French aristocrats began amassing blue and white Chinese porcelain from the moment it began to be imported; eventually they possessed many magnificent pieces and frequently displayed them on silver or gold mountings.

Today, blue and white can still be collected here and there, piece by piece, without spending too much money. It offers many options for beautiful table settings. For example, you can mix non-matching plates of the same shade of blue with different patterns; or mix blues of many different shades from pale to dark; or simply use one specific pattern. The possibilities are endless.

Charming blue and white earthenware services, the everyday tableware of our grandmothers, can still be purchased for bargain prices. But as soon as you go back to the seventeenth and eighteenth centuries, values rise very steeply. And it is out of the question to eat from such dishes since they are collector's items.

2.

3.

4.

2.

3.

4.

Single Color, Embossed, and Openwork Services

Single color ceramics show the quality of their paste and allow sculpted patterns. There is often a simplicity and sophistication about them. Their most charming examples are the green, brown, and sunshine-yellow wares of the south of France or the snow white and gold filigree of Paris and Limoges porcelain.

The Simplicity of Single Color

While craftsmen in faience seem to have had a marked preference for polychrome decoration, in the mid-eighteenth century, the factories of Saint-Clement, Strasbourg, and Marseilles were producing white earthenware—sometimes heightened with gold filigree—that was also of excellent quality. Moreover many fine single-color dishes with scrolled, curving, or multifoil shapes emerged from the kilns of Moustiers and its neighbor Varages, and also from Hautecombe, next to Lac du Bourget, and the potteries of France's south.

In the first half of the nineteenth century, manufacturers in eastern France and the Paris region developed an especially fine paste called pipe clay. It was a beautiful cream color, so beautiful that patterns were often not deemed necessary for it—a transparent covering was enough. In this way, vast numbers of round and octagonal plates, sometimes with gadroon edges according to the style of the period, were produced and sold at very low prices. At the end of the century, many faience potteries produced utilitarian single-color crockery for daily use, finely enameled and in every pastel color, while porcelain manufacturers opted for white, pure and simple.

Pont-aux-Choux Cream

When fine faience was invented in England, it created a revolution in the industry. French potteries set about imitating it, and in 1740 the *Manufacture Royale des Terres de France, à l'imitation de celles d'Angleterre* was founded in rue Saint-Sebastien in the Charonne quarter of Paris. This earthenware factory was better known as Pont-aux-choux for its proximity to a bridge crossing a ditch where cabbages—*choux* in French—were grown. For fifteen years it produced cream-colored "English" ware of very high quality. Its shapes were largely taken from silverware;

1. Octagonal, boss-beaded Empire plates.

2 to 4. Pont-aux-Choux faience, late 18th century. Round soup tureen (2.), Tureen platter (3.), and oval soup tureen on its platter (4.).

1.

tled ware. Its ornamentation, like that of Pont-aux-Choux, was expressed in reliefs only, with the potter functioning as a sculptor. Its principal pattern was rice grain, but it also used vegetables and flowers. Castellet, a town neighboring Apt, was distinctive for its small flowerlets with five, nine, or twelve petals, its reeds, and its scrolls. As for the shapes, these too were strongly influenced by silverware. The plates were profiled, the platters oblong, and the other pieces covered in knobs in the shapes of animals and fruits, with branchlike lugs and handles. As time passed, these shapes became more and more spare.

The plates were octagonal, with gadroon edges and Greek borders, and rosettes and acanthus leaves took the place of more natural looking flowers. By the end of the nineteenth century, Apt had to compete not only with Sarreguemines but also with English faience and Limoges porcelain: and in the early twentieth century, its production ceased altogether. Other centers like Uzès, Vallauris, Aubagne, and Fréjus also produced fine yellow, cream, or white ware, while Dieulefit maintained a predilection for yellow-green and black.

Openwork and Braided

The small earthenware center at Langeais, in the Touraine region of France, made a specialty of openwork faience. Not only did it produce baskets with movable handles, decorated with vines, cherries, strawberry plants, pears, ivy, oak leaves, and acorns, it also manufactured plates with braided or perforated rims. This original technique was copied by Niderviller and Marseilles in the second half of the nineteenth century and subsequently by Malicorne after 1924. The woven faience baskets of Moustiers and Uzès were also famous, as were those of Hautecombe.

White Porcelain

Following the discovery of kaolin at Saint-Yrieux in 1735, two main centers—Paris and Limoges—began producing very high

it carried as colored decoration only very lightly worked reliefs of branches, checkerboards, and rice grains. The tops of Pont-aux-Choux tureen covers were shaped like flowers or vegetables, the pouring spouts were made like small branches, and the handles on the bigger dishes were in the form of animal heads.

Yellow Faience from the South of France

Apt, in the Vaucluse, was already a center for pottery before the Romans arrived there. But it was in the eighteen and above all in the nineteenth century that the town became famous for the quality and delicacy of its earthenware. Indeed some people think that stoneware was invented in Apt, and not in England. Whatever the case, Apt faience is highly original, especially in its color: Apt was devoted to yellow in all its nuances and also produced very fine marbled or mot-

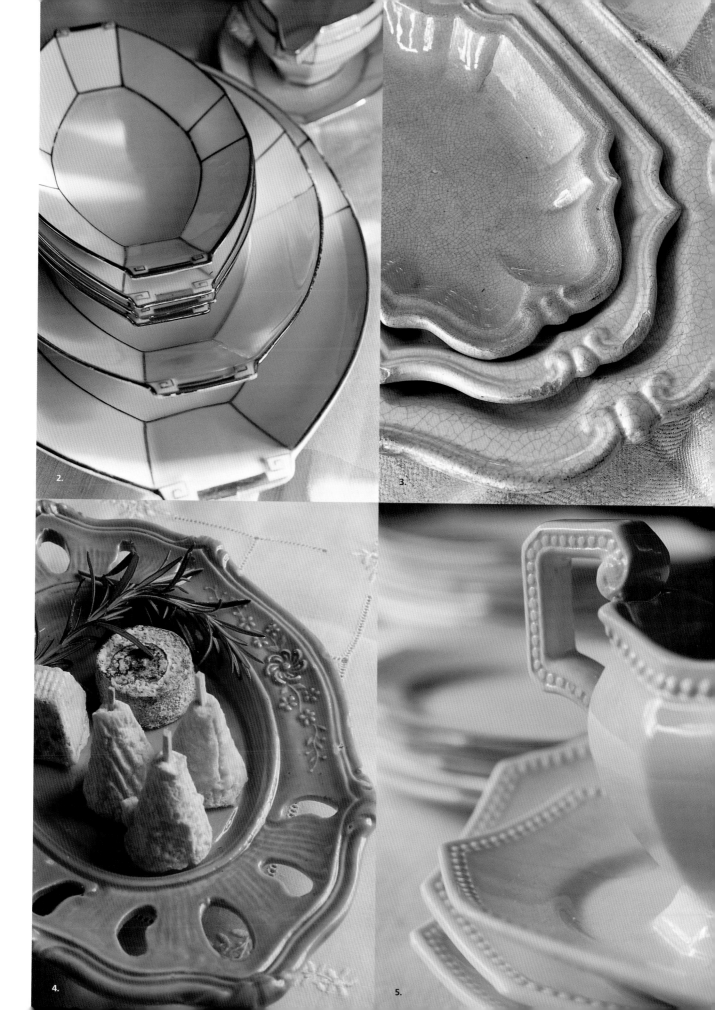

2.

3.

4.

5.

1.

1. Porcelain plates, with gilded edges and monogram.

2. Perforated plate with ornamentations in relief. Manufacture de Creil et Montereau, late 19th century.

3. Wedgwood porcelain plate with rim decorated in relief, 19th century.

4. Porcelain cake plate with string trompe l'oeil pattern, 19th century.

5. Shiny biscuit porcelain with fruit decoration, a copy of *Impératrice* pattern by R. Haviland and C. Parlon.

quality porcelain. Paris was distinguished for the whiteness of its paste, its fine grain, and its perfect vitrification—many white dinnerware with simple gold trim were produced there—but in the end, Limoges won the ascendancy. The dynasties of Allaud, Tharaud, and Baignol established themselves as the masters of porcelain in Limoges after the Revolution, slowly perfecting their techniques. Etienne Baignol produced pure white china with gold edging; Tharaud worked on the contrasts between matte and enameled porcelain; and Allaud and his sons developed their distinctive broad bands of gold.

In the second half of the nineteenth century, the Pouyat family produced a paste of such whiteness and delicacy that it was baptized *mousseline* (muslin). Perforations were cut into the paste with a stylus to emphasize the happy contrast of transparency and opaqueness: these services were known as *grain de riz* (rice grain).

The traditional ornament craftsman found himself transformed into a sculptor, endowing pure porcelain with foliage and sheaves of wheat, and manipulating the contrast between biscuit and enamel: an example is the "Ceres" service, created in 1855 by the sculptor Paul Comolera.

Little by little, the white began to be trimmed and decorated with gold, with simple fillets, hound's tooth patterns, and florets. Figures festooned with flower garlands, ribbons, or knots adorned the white marriage services that became popular with the bourgeoisie as the very name of Limoges became synonymous with whiteness.

TIPS FOR COLLECTORS

Pont-aux-Choux pieces are very rare today, and their price reflects this fact. They are collector's items.

Older pieces from Apt or Castellet are also collector's items, but later imitations and even contemporary pieces made in the traditional method by potteries in the south of France are not without interest. Single-color, pipe-clay plates are also very charming, notably octagonal ones. But since pipe clay is a poor quality material, many items made with it will be scratched or stained, and their prices have stayed low. Gold and white Paris or Limoges porcelain is not hard to find, but with these pieces, it is important to check the state of the gold.

2.

3.

4.

5.

Illustrated Printed Plates

Illustrated plates, which were mass-produced in the nineteenth century, are still found in large numbers. They can be used as dessert plates or combined with flat plates with matching colors. In any case, their printed riddles, scenes from military life, and simple jokes have an old-fashioned charm that is irresistible.

History

Who invented the process? The experts disagree. Sadler and Green of Liverpool are known to have applied engraving to the decoration of earthenware beginning in 1752. In France, Francois-Antoine Legros d'Anisy opened a factory exclusively devoted to printing plates and faience works such as Creil and Choisy, and even Sèvres employed him to decorate their products. The engravings were black and, sometimes, dark brown in color. Legros d'Anisy was given a silver medal at the 1819 Exhibition.

Before long, all the major stoneware manufacturers had set up their own printing shops. Creil was the first to use the process on an industrial scale.

Gazettes and Fables

Until about 1837, the designs were monochrome: blue, brown, or black were simply applied to white stoneware or to a paste colored using metal oxides (yellow backgrounds, essentially produced by Creil or more rarely green). Thereafter the plates became bicolored, with one impression for the center, in black for example, and another for the borders in blue, green, or red. Eventually the ware became multicolored, an effect that could be obtained by stenciling colors on to printed faience.

Prior to about 1830, themes remained sober, and patterns rarely differed from those of hand-decorated plates—the motif being centered in the middle of the plate while a border of acanthus leaves, oak leaves, and flowers ran around the rim. Mythology was one of the principal sources of inspiration, with scenes from the lives of heroes or gods surrounded by a frieze of palm leaves. The designers also drew freely on history; the troubadour fashion—launched by Charles X's daughter-in-law, the Duchess of Berry, with designs inspired by the works of Sir Walter Scott—was very popular for a time. The kings of France, the Revolution, and Napoleon were other favorites, as was geography, with sober views of towns, villages, and monuments. This was also the time when somewhat less serious themes such as La Fontaine's fables, songs and riddles first made their appearance.

Conundrums, Novels, and Songs

During the reign of Louis-Philippe, plates were loaded with a riot of colors, including bright yellow, orange, blue, mauve, and brown. The rims were covered with complicated patterns of fruits, bouquets, checks, and lambrequins, while the center was filled with humorous or fantastic decorations. But serious historical themes, geography, feats of arms, and portraits of great men were also much favored.

The Second Empire saw the return of the rococo style and more muted colors. Plates appeared with contours that imitated flower petals; their rims bore light

2.

3.

4.

1. Faience soup tureen and soup plate from an archbishop's table service. Manufacture de Choisy-le-Roi, 1850. This type of service inspired decorations that were later printed and mass-produced.

2. Blue and sepia illustrated plate, leopard motif, from a set of wild animal designs.

3. Faience plate with rim decorated in relief, representing a pastoral scene, Second Empire period.

4. Blue and sepia illustrated plate: *Le duc d'Orléans aux portes de fer.*

1.

1. Study of a monogram for a table service. Atelier Emile Gallé, 1888.

2. The entire bowl of this platter is occupied by its illustration of a coronet entwined with ornamental foliage. Rim is decorated in relief, 19th century.

patterns of white-on-white relief, representing stitching, foliage, or basketwork. The decoration of the middle was in black, sepia, or gray, usually in medallions. Often the patterns referred to great inventions, works of art, Universal Exhibitions, or military achievements. Great novels of the period, such as *The Mysteries of Paris* or *The Count of Monte Cristo*, would be compressed into six plates. Songs appeared with one plate per couple. A humorous vein was widely exploited, with satires, charades, jokes, riddles, conundrums, and proverbs galore.

Toward the end of the nineteenth century, printed plates ceased to be merely black and white, and crockery was again flooded with colors. Dishes also became larger, echoing the satirical papers of the times and glorifying heroes and politicians. The patriotic theme—principally that of Alsace-Lorraine—was among the most popular; it was invariably handled humorously, as were scenes from military life. Religious iconography was also much appreciated, with plates serving as pages of the catechism. Also during this period, the first advertising plates appeared on the market.

After the Second World War, there was less interest in illustrated plates, even though themes such as the Tour de France, automobiles, and planes persisted.

Major Potteries

The Montereau works, in the Seine-et-Marne, was founded in 1745 and was among the oldest of its type. In 1775 it took the title of *Manufacture de la Reine* (The Queen's Pottery). The high quality of its paste rivaled that of Sarreguemines at the Exhibition of Industrial Products of 1801–1802.

The Creil manufacturer, on the banks of the River Oise, was founded in 1797 but did not really begin to function full blast until 1802. It became famous with the arrival of Charles-Gaspard Alexandre Saint-Cricq Casaux, who won a number of gold medals at various exhibitions of industrial products.

In 1819, the owner of Creil, M. Saint-Cricq Casaux, bought out the Montereau potteries. He began by renting them to a company run by Louis Leboeuf and Etienne Thibault in 1825, before merging everything into the *Societe des Faienceries de Creil et de Montereau*. In 1895, Creil closed down altogether and moved all its assets to Montereau. In 1920, Montereau went on to buy out Choisy-le-Roi, which ceased production in 1934. Montereau itself finally closed down in 1955.

In 1772, Joseph Fabry and the brothers Nicolas and Augustin Jacoby founded a faience works at Sarreguemines. In 1778 they recruited a young Bavarian, Francois-Paul Ultzschneider, who had worked for the famous English firm of Wedgwood. After the War of 1870, Sarreguemines was annexed to Germany with the rest of Lorraine and was forced to pay customs duty on the products it exported to France; whereupon it started a new factory within France at Digoin in Saone-et-Loire. From that time, all the output of Sarreguemines bore the names of both potteries.

TIPS FOR COLLECTORS

There are many delightful possibilities open to collectors of this kind of faience, whether they approach it by individual pottery, period, color, or theme. The most widely produced series are still very reasonably priced, but it is usually best to purchase items one by one, since complete series are always much more expensive. Currently, the most sought after names are Creil and Gien. Above all, look for pieces without any cracks or defects.

2.

3.

4.

Flowers

Whether presented in simple lines or in sophisticated bouquets, naturalistic or stylized, flowers are the all-time favorite themes of ceramic decoration. Stylized flowers were already a feature of Ancient Egyptian pottery, as they were for medieval Islamic earthenware and ancient Chinese porcelain. In Europe, it was in the wake of Linnaeus, the Swedish botanist, that the eighteenth-century vogue for naturalism came about, bringing with it a pronounced taste for floral patterns.

The German Flowers of Meissen

The first European factory to feature flowers was Meissen, a village of Saxe in Germany where, in 1713, the chemist Friedrich Boettger discovered the secret of Chinese porcelain—that its paste was made with kaolin. In the 1720s and 1730s, Johan Gregor Herold created a floral decoration, *Indianische Blumen* ("Indian flowers"), influenced by Japanese asymmetry and coloring. This design was immediately copied by most of the other European factories. Ten years later, *Deutsche Blumen* ("German flowers") appeared; these were more naturalistic in conception and were sometimes surrounded by insects. The patterns were quickly taken up by Vincennes/Sèvres, which produced excellent versions of them.

The **fleurs fines** of Strasbourg

The invention of slow firing is attributed to Paul-Antoine Hannong, whose father, Charles-Francois, created the Strasbourg pottery workshop in 1709. With this new technique, the Hannong factory made a specialty of what was called *fleurs fines*, notably consisting of bouquets made up

of "swirling roses." These roses were often round, with a view straight into the heart of the blossom and its petals. The tones were invariably subtle, contrasting the carmine of the petals with the dark green of the thick stems. There were also bouquets made up of slender tulips with cornflowers and buttercups. These floral patterns were copied all over France, especially by Niderviller, Strasbourg's neighbor.

Marseilles Bouquets

The Marseilles region was another great center for earthenware, which was renowned for its flower patterns. The most celebrated potteries there were the ones founded by the Clérissy brothers at Saint-Jean-du-Désert in 1679, Joseph Fauchier, and Veuve Perrin. Toward 1750, these names began producing delicate floral decors, fired at low heat against white or yellow backgrounds. The Marseilles bouquets often represented roses and tulips blended with meadow flowers and handled naturalistically. They were the inspiration for other potteries all over the south, especially Moustiers.

1. Hand-painted porcelain, characterized by freshness of design and color.

2 to 4. Three faience patterns from the Utzschneider works at Sarreguemines: *Geranium*, circa 1890 (2.), roast meat platter, circa 1900 (3.), and *Pompadour*, floral decoration, 1880 (4.).

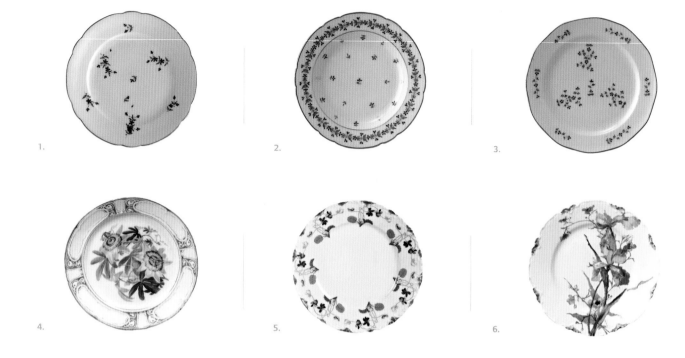

1.   2.   3.

4.   5.   6.

1 to 3. Different examples of cornflower patterns on the bowls and rims of plates. Manufacture de la Reine, 18th century.

4. A romantic flower pattern by Barbarin for *Vieux* Limoges service. Haviland, 1855.

5. Decorations of violets by Léonce Ribière, for Empress Eugénie. Haviland, 1901.

6. Bright yellow *fleurs parisiennes* by Girardin. Haviland, 1885.

7. Flowers and gilded motifs on the rims of an 18th-century-style cake service.

8. A graceful flower pattern, delicately outlined in sepia.

9. Moss roses hand-painted on porcelain, with acid greens and blues.

10. Flowering roses overflow from the rims of these early-20th-century cake plates into the wells.

Thistles and Potato Flowers

Other, less famous potteries were also creating original flower patterns. This was the case of Meillonas, near Bourg-la-Reine. This firm, founded in 1759, won fame in 1759 with its hot-fired "manganese pink" pattern. (The same pattern made a name for the Tres-cloitres works in Grenoble.) Meillonas was equally at home with the use of slow-fired dcorations, dominated by naturalistic stereotypical flowers.

Samadet, a small village in the Landes department made a specialty of finely executed flower designs, such as blue-hued thistles and potato flowers. "Samadet roses" were very original: unrealistic and stylized, their blossoms were round with straight cut, lacy petals and stalks that were dead straight or studded with thorns.

Flowers on Soft-Paste Porcelain

Soft-paste (kaolin-free) porcelain had appeared in Rouen in 1673 around the same time as stoneware, as a result of Edmé Poterat's work. However it really came into its own with the products of Saint-Cloud, Chantilly, Mennecy, Sceaux, and of course Vincennes and Sèvres, at the beginning of the eighteenth century. Chantilly made a specialty of floral patterns. After representations of strawberry flowers in the Kakiemon style, more natural-looking flowers predominated, such as bunches of roses, peonies, and primulas. By the end of the eighteenth century, Chantilly was specializing in stylized sprays of flowers in blue tones notably *à la brindille* (sprigs of heather) and *à l'oeillet* (carnations), which were echoed by Orléans, Arras, Sèvres, and the factories of Paris and southern and eastern France, and also inspired the decorators of Creil and Montereau.

Fifteen years after it was founded in 1735, the pottery at Sceaux invented a stylized bouquet consisting of two flowers side by side with a twig bearing small round blossoms between the stalks. Sometimes there would be one flower only, purple in color with garish green leaves. Mennecy, founded in 1737, specialized in bouquets of roses, peonies, and tulips in pink tones.

7.

8.

9.

10.

1.

1. A rotund tea set decorated with fresh, bright flowers.

2. Scattered flowers on a porcelain plate from Paris.

3. Bouquet of flowers in the center of a fragile faience plate. Manufacture de Niderviller, circa 1760.

4. Hand-painted flowers on these 18th-century, soft-paste porcelain is the epitome of delicacy and precision.

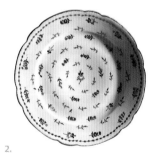

2.

3.

The Roses and Cornflowers of Sèvres

The Vincennes pottery, founded in 1738, became the *Manufacture Royale* in 1752, under the aegis of Louis XV and his mistress Mme. de Pompadour. It began by imitating Saxony porcelain, notably with its "German flower" patterns. In 1756, Vincennes moved to Sèvres where, with its royal privileges, it was able to dominate the porcelain industry of the day. The factory itself was made up of a number of different workshops: paste makers, repairers, modelers, sculptors, gilders, and painters. In the painters' shop, some of the craftsmen specialized entirely in flower patterns.

After 1760, Sèvres adopted the pattern of *roses et feuillages* ("roses and foliage"); this consisted of small simple rose blossoms scattered across a white background. This became a lasting standard for Sèvres and was copied by Paris and Limoges.

In 1781, Marie-Antoinette, who had a passion for pinks and cornflowers, commissioned a service from the royal pottery known as *guirlandes de barbeaux* ("garlands of cornflowers"). Painted by Choisy and gilded by Chauveau, this service is produced to this day by the former *Manufacture Royale*. Cornflowers immediately joined roses as a predominant theme in porcelain plate patterns.

They were included in the inventories of most of the Paris manufactures of hard-paste porcelain, in scattered patterns, friezes, bouquets, and medallions, and were equally popular with the faience makers of eastern France and Savoy.

Miniature Roses of Limoges

The early years of Limoges were notable for their charming, somewhat simple polychrome flower patterns, either gathered in bouquets at the center of the plate and distributed in sprays around its edge or in the style of Louis XVI, with pink or blue cornflowers and green ribbons. Limoges copied the miniature roses of Sèvres, which then became "Limoges roses." Flowers were omnipresent, in the form of tulips and flat flowerets of the wallpaper type, and other floral patterns that imitated Chantilly, Sèvres, and Mennecy. These patterns were sometimes rimmed with *dents-de-loup* festoons.

1.

Flowerets and Convolvulus

After 1850, flowers by the million blossomed on all forms of china and earthenware. Simple, unpretentious flowerets—roses and poppies—were painted on everyday faience, while more finely wrought flowers were devised for the table services of the middle class—essentially by Sarreguemines, Creil, Gien, Longwy, and Montereau, whose flower services of blue convolvulus against a white background became a great classic. At Niderviller, which had begun producing porcelain by this time, the patterns were a riot of red flowers, ranging from pale pink to dark red and multicolored bouquets. Occasionally there would be a new version of an eighteenth-century Sèvres pattern that came dangerously close to affectation, with flowers and gilding against a background of solid turquoise or pink.

Limoges and the Vogue for Japan

In 1842, David Haviland, the American importer of soft porcelain, was sufficiently impressed by the quality of Limoges china to found a decoration workshop of his own there. Within ten years he had his own factory in the town, producing porcelain exclusively for export to the United States. His sons Charles and Theodore then started a creative studio at Auteuil, managed by the painter Felix Bracquemond. It was the period when French artists were discovering Japanese prints and the works of Hokusai. The *fleurs et rubans* ("flowers and ribbons") pattern devised by Braquemond in 1879, along with Pallandres' 1883 *fleurs parisiennse* ("Parisian flowers") were characteristic of this trend.

Back in Limoges, the painter Georges Le Feure and the architect Edward Colonna came up with an art nouveau pattern for porcelain based on stylized vegetable motifs, many of them in relief and enhanced with pastel tones against a pale background. The painter Léonce Ribière designed two very pretty services: *Les Nymphéas* and *Caroline* on the theme of Parma violets. The latter was given by Theodore Haviland in 1901 to the Empress Eugénie, then aged seventy five.

TIPS FOR COLLECTORS

There is a very wide and varied choice of faience and hard-paste porcelain on the secondhand market.

Gien, Creil, and Montereau are all abundantly available. Nor are prices particularly high for Limoges flower-patterned services, bearing in mind that in this case, a complete service usually costs less than pieces acquired one by one. Series of dessert or cake plates in fine Limoges flower patterns can be found everywhere, selling at bargain prices. But plates designed by Suzanne Lalique, Jean Dufy, or Van Dongen are at a premium.

Japanese-style or art nouveau motifs have become rarities and are costly—as are older pieces of all kinds, which now tend to be confined to display cases.

2.

3.

1.

Barbotine Plates

These dazzling plates, with naturalistic motifs drawn from art nouveau, are like rays of sunshine on the table. They were only produced for about fifty years, but their blossoming patterns, which have often been copied but never equaled, have lost none of their appeal.

2.

3.

4.

Barbotine

The original barbotine was a mix of clay and water used for molding a shape or sticking together the different elements of a piece of faience. The French gave the same name to a type of brightly colored, relief-patterned earthenware, which was produced between 1870 and the outbreak of the Second World War and which the English called *majolica*.

Strictly speaking, barbotine is a stoneware paste that lends itself particularly well to molding and delicate relief. Barbotine plates were made on the wheel or in molds. After drying, they were fired in the kiln at about 200°F, before being covered in a transparent lead enamel mixed with colored oxides. After that, they were refired at 1500°F.

The first French barbotines appeared around 1860. They were the work of Charles-Jean Avisseau, who was inspired by the work of Bernard Palissy. Arriseau's unveiling of his products at the London industrial exhibition aroused the admiration of Europe, and other great ceramicists flocked to his workshop in Tours. The fashion for barbotine was launched with the support of Napoleon III's niece, Princess Mathilde. Thereafter it was produced on a large scale until the 1920s, when it went into a gradual decline.

Naturalistic Decoration

Barbotine vases, planters, flower stands, jugs, asparagus plates, and shellfish dishes were adorned with dazzling naturalistic motifs and colors, and by 1880, barbotine dessert plates and fruit dishes were being produced in great numbers. Sometimes the plates and dishes were set into brass-wired mounts, which allowed them to be transformed into fruit or bread baskets.

When barbotine first appeared, neo-Renaissance style was in fashion, with acanthus leaves, lambrequins, and scrolls symmetrically positioned in relation to a central point. After this came the Japanese style, with its cherry blooms, bamboos, and birds freely represented anywhere on the piece; these in turn were superseded by the naturalistic, stylized patterns and flowers of art nouveau.

The principal themes of barbotine ware were leaves (ferns, ivy, and wild roses), vegetables (asparagus, artichokes, radishes, eggplants, and leeks), fruits (strawberries, pears, grapes, plums, and lemons), and flowers (daisies, sunflowers, roses, peonies, cornflowers, dahlias, violets, lilacs, and pansies).

From Sarreguemines to Vallauris

Sarraguemines was probably the most important pottery center in eastern France, employing about two thousand workers in the 1870s. The kilns of Sarreguemines steadily increased their production of barbotine ware, particularly after 1910, with each original becoming available in several versions and colors.

Lunéville, which was founded in 1720, earned the title of *Manufacture Royale* in 1772, under the protection of Stanislas Leszczynski. In the eighteenth century, Lunéville faience was celebrated for its quality as it moved from stanniferous earthenware to stoneware. Its production

1. Decorative plate with fruits and leaves in relief. Manufacture de Longchamp, late 19th century.

2. Plate with vine-leaf design. Manufacture de Sarreguemines, late 19th century.

3. Rooster jug. Manufacture d'Orchies, late 19th century.

4. The deep, rich colors of an asparagus and artichoke plate.

1.

of barbotine ware was substantial and notable for its bright colors.

In the nineteenth century, Lunéville's subsidiary, Saint-Clément, turned out considerable quantities of plates bearing the popular rooster motif, while its extravagantly art nouveau barbotine ware differed from that of its rivals on account of its subtle patterning and the delicacy of its colors.

The exact origins of earthenware production at Longwy are not known, except that a pottery works was started there by the Boch family in 1801. From 1865 onward, Longwy focused on the technique of cloissonne enamel that was to make it famous. The Longwy works also produced shaded enamel and barbotine ware of very delicate manufacture, which were frequently of a single color and inspired by the East.

Clairefontaine, in the Franche-Comté near Vesoul, was known for its fine monochrome green and bicolored pink and white ware, while Salins produced large numbers of well-made plates with sophisticated flower and checkerboard patterns. The Longchamp pottery, founded very late in the nineteenth century, was known for its vases and plates decorated with fruits and flowers in relief.

There were also a number of potteries in northern France that produced substantial quantities of barbotine ware—notably Saint-Amand-les-Eaux, Onnaing near Valenciennes (famous for its jugs featuring different animals and public figures), Orchies, Dèvres, and Five-Lille.

The barbotine of Choisy, in the southern suburbs of Paris, and of Gien are perhaps the most beautiful of all. The celebrated green Choisy plate with its vine-leaf pattern was reproduced in the 1950s for Primavera.

Last but not least was the production of the Massier family—Delphin, his brother Clément, and his cousin Jérome—in Vallauris, a small village in the Alpes Maritimes. This famous workshop began by making fine monochrome glazes with Renaissance motifs in tones of turquoise, carmine, and green before graduating to naturalistic art nouveau barbotine ware

between 1860 and 1910. Their dessert plates and fruit dishes took the form of open daisies, pansies, and sunflowers.

Rubelles Plates

In 1838, Baron de Bourgoing went into partnership with Alexis de Tremblay to start a pottery at Rubelles, on the outskirts of Melun. In 1842, he invented *émail ombrant* ("shaded glazing"), the technique that consisted of stamping a pattern into stoneware paste and covering it with a layer of translucent colored glaze. The relief emerged under this glaze as the liquid settled into the hollows and the patterns stood out in lighter tones.

Landscapes, nature scenes, coats of arms, a variety of animals, and above all fruits (pears, cherries, grapes, red currants, black currants, lemons, quinces, and olives) were centered in the bottom of a round or multifoil plate, whose rim might be perforated, woven, or molded. The colors have a peculiar depth; cobalt blue, rusty brown, and a fine chrome yellow. The Rubelles workshop closed down in 1858, but its patterns continued to be imitated by Sarreguemines, Choisy, Longwy, Clairefontaine, Salins, Gien, Creil, and, above all, Le Mée-sur-Seine.

TIPS FOR COLLECTORS

Recently there has been a revival of interest in barbotine ware, and with it came an increase in the numbers of counterfeits.
Lunéville, Saint-Clément, and Orchies are still affordable; prices for Choisy are on the rise; and Vallauris is heavily—and deservedly—sought after.
If you intend to use barbotine plates, it is best to select those that are in mint condition. Worn glazing makes the plates porous, which absorbs marks and stains.
As a general rule, the heavier the relief of a pattern, the older the piece.
Out of all ceramics, barbotine is the one that best lends itself to restoration. This has its advantages, but also its drawbacks, since the restoration work is often hard to detect.

2.

3.

4.

5.

SERVEWARE

Many dishes and receptacles that were well-known in their time are simply no longer made today. Such is the case of the celebrated eighteenth-century à oille stew pot, and even of the tureen, which today has a different shape to that of its ancestor. Gastronomic habits have also changed, and of course each category of food has its corresponding dish. Thus the soup tureen, a utensil much used in our grandparents' times, was progressively abandoned in the second half of the twentieth century when people consumed less and less soup—though today it is coming back strongly. Barbotine asparagus plates, bright and redolent of spring, are once again in favor. Other specific items that are less commonly used are fruit plates, fruit stands, and delicate plates for cake and tart.

And then there are all the other indispensable items of every shape and size. We buy them on impulse for their patterns and colors. With their blend of beauty and usefulness, they exemplify an ideal of refinement that enchants the aesthete and the gourmet alike.

1.

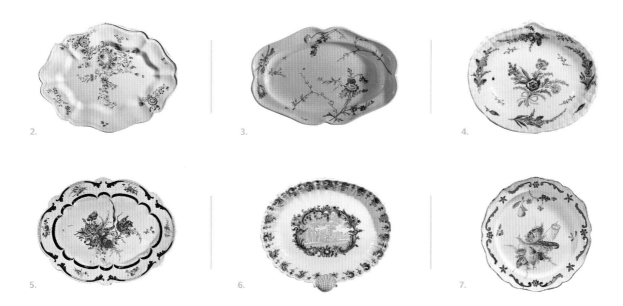

Dishes from the Past

Old dishes and bowls, whose shapes have changed little over the centuries, have failed to compete effectively with the sheer diversity of modern products. In a sense they are the poor relations of the table. But perhaps the moment has come to restore them to their rightful place in the order; prices are low at present, and there are abundant pieces on offer.

Evolving Forms and Shapes

Toward the end of the eighteenth century, dishes differed little, except that each type existed in several sizes, sometimes up to twelve different sizes for the same pattern. They were generally less ornate than the equivalent "shaped" pieces. Under the French Regency, octagonal and hexagonal dishes had lightly gadrooned edges. Around 1730, the classic patterns were round and profiled, with five or six lobes; or oval, with six or eight. These types of dishes have remained current to this day. Under Louis XV, profiled dishes were covered in opulent and asymmetrical patterns, whereas in his son's reign there was a return to classicism with more symmetrical designs. The nineteenth century saw a return to older styles and rococo romanticism, with the trend for nature-

inspired design prevailing by the close of the century. In the 1920s, art nouveau naturalism gave way to the sober, modernist style of art deco.

Specific Serving Dishes

While we acknowledge the enormous round venison platters of old, which were without contours and had narrow molded edges, it must be said that few serving dishes to speak of appeared before the nineteenth century. Beef and roast platters were equipped with detachable perforated drainers with four feet set in their raised rims. Big fish platters, which had similar perforated drainers, invariably caused a sensation when they arrived at the table: "The cold fish is laid on a long dish covered with an embroidered napkin, its edges encircled by flowers, periwin-

ETYMOLOGY

The word "platter" derives from the Greek *platos*, meaning broad." In 1328, the word *plat* in French designated a piece of crockery with a flat bottom, later expanding its meaning to cover the concave dishes used to transport food from kitchen to table and present it to best advantage.

Preceding pages:

Left: Cream-colored faience soup tureen. Manufacture de Sarreguemines, 19th century.
Right: Empire-style sauceboat, in the shape of an antique Roman lamp.

1. Concave platter and rectangular platter, silver-plated, 1930s.

2 to 7. Oval platters and round platters with contoured edges. From various Marseilles potteries, Louis XV period.

1.

3.

1. Round silver stew dishes with handles on either side, copied from various styles of the past, 19th century.

2. Square silver dishes, copied from various styles of the past, 19th century.

3. Hors d'oeuvre dishes of various shapes. The main structure is silver-plated metal, and the compartments for the hors d'oeuvres are made of crystal. Christofle designs, 19th century.

4. Soup tureen and typical Provencal platters, 17th and 18th century.

5. Cream-colored faience terrines from Lunéville.

kles, primroses, and nasturtiums," says a 1925 guide to good living. Boiled beef dishes, by contrast, incorporated compartments for accompanying vegetables.

Materials

Traditionally, serving dishes were made of brass, silver, or vermeil; metal was usually preferable to ceramic because it did not break. But faience and porcelain makers eventually replaced their metalworking colleagues by borrowing their forms and molds. After 1830, round and oval serving dishes of different sizes made of earthenware and porcelain became as much a feature of table settings as the soup tureen or the vegetable dish. In today's jargon, they were "coordinated" with the rest of the table service. Nevertheless the invention of silver plate led to a substantial new production of dishes that generally imitated the shapes of the past. It was not unusual at the end of the nineteenth century for a household to possess both silver and ceramic serving dishes.

TIPS FOR COLLECTORS

There is little demand at present for old serving dishes, and as a result there are plenty of bargains around. If the dish or platter is solid silver, then you must take account as always of the hallmark, the signature, the quality of the work, and the condition of the piece. If it is silver plate, choose with particular care because dishes of this kind were mass-produced and can be found everywhere—though if they were made by a famous firm like Christofle, there may be added value.

There is no shortage of ceramic serving dishes on the market. Their shapes may be commonplace, but good patterns and colors more than make up for this.

Carefully check the condition of the dish—no crack or chip is ever acceptable.

Bowls and Old-Fashioned Platters

Terrines, stew pots, and porringers; these old-fashioned-sounding dishes are no longer much present on our tables. Instead they are kept on shelves or in display cabinets. Nevertheless, their former glory more than justifies the interest taken in them by lovers of the art of the table.

Sauceboats are rapidly becoming collector's items, while the good old soup tureen is now returning with a vengeance after a period in the wilderness. This is entirely because they are so attractive, with their elegant shapes and reassuring bulges. Some people use them at table; others set them around the house as planters or wall pockets.

The **pot à oille**

Oille was a Spanish stew of various meats and vegetables, first mentioned in 1671. It derived its name from the Spanish *olla*, meaning a kind of cooking pot. *Oille* arrived in France about the time of Louis XIV's marriage to the Infanta Maria Teresa. In the eighteenth century, before the invention of the soup tureen, the *pot à oille* was the most important dish on the French table—a round, deep dish with an inside component that could be removed to make its contents easier to serve. It was between 7³/₄ to 11 inches in diameter, had four legs, two side handles, and a convex lid, and rested on a big stand known as a *dormant* ("sleeper"). It was accompanied by a round-bowled ladle. Under Louis XIV, the *pot à oille* was a sumptuous item, richly ornate and always made of silver. Indeed, it was the leading actor of the first course, which consisted of boiled meats and soup and often had an identical twin. The most famous *pots à oille* were made by Delaunay, Germain, Balzac, Meissonnier, Roettiers, and Auguste. Stoneware manufacturers copied it in their turn, with Pont-aux-Choux producing *pots à oille* inspired by metalwork, Joseph Hannong in Strasbourg creating trompe l'oeil cab-

bage patterns for them, and Veuve Perrin in Marseilles devising exquisitely delicate decorations for their outer surfaces. Under Louis XVI, the *pot à oille* became heavier and with the empire it took a more wide-mouthed form. It more or less vanished after the Restoration, at which time the soup tureen and the vegetable dish took its place.

The Terrine

The terrine, as its name suggests, was originally an earthenware dish used for stewing meats. Around 1720, this dish made the transition from the kitchen to the dining table and became just as refined as the *pot à oille*. Stoneware examples of these early terrines do exist, but most tended to be made of metal. The terrine was similar to the *pot à oille* inasmuch as it rested on four feet, had its own stand, was fitted with a removable cover, and sometimes contained another receptacle. But it was lower and oval in shape, not round (the oval was between 11 and 15³/₄ inches in length). The handles and lid were often decorated with hunting scenes. Its uses were various; stews were not the only dishes served in it. It had its own serving ladle, whose bowl was also oval.

1. Stoneware soup tureen, Empire period.

2 and 3. *Pots à oille*, slow-fired faience. Manufactures de Meillonas (2.) and de Hannong, in Strasbourg style (3.).

4 to 6. Slow-fired faience terrines. Manufactures de Marseille, 1760–1770.

1. 2. 3.

1. Louis XV hot-fired faience porringer. Manufacture de Moustiers, circa 1750.

2. Polychrome porringer, design inspired by the Imari Japanese style. Manufacture de Saint-Cloud, 18th century.

3. Porcelain porringer with "Three Graces" design. Manufacture de Limoges, 18th century.

4. Designs for silver sauceboats with either one or two pourers, copies of ancient oil-lamp designs.

5. Stoneware sauceboat with a single pourer and gadroon design. Manufacture de Sarreguemines, Empire period.

6. Faience sauceboat with printed *Flora* design. Manufacture de Sarreguemines, circa 1880.

4.

The Individual Porringers

The ancestor of our own concave plates, the porringer was a small flat-bottomed bowl whose shape harked back to the Middle Ages. It was one of the first individual containers to appear on European tables. In the seventeenth century, it incorporated two side grips, a removable lid to keep its contents hot, and the platter on which it stood. The most famous French porringer belonged to the Dauphin, Louis XIV's son. It dates from 1692 and is made of vermeil, with gilded side handles decorated with shells and dolphins.

The porringer was particularly well adapted to nursing women and to those in poor health who could only eat gruel and was a common gift to a newborn, presented in a leather pouch. Strasbourg specialized in the manufacture of silver porringers. Other factories produced many variations of it: for example, the famous Hannong porringers, also of Strasbourg, came in the shape of ducks, turkeys, geese, and vegetables.

TIPS FOR COLLECTORS

Pots à oille and terrines, whether made of porcelain or solid silver, are rare collector's items.
Strasbourg porringers made by Alerti, Imlin, or Kirstein are equally sought after.

The Sauceboat or Gravy Boat

The shape of the sauceboat has changed little over the centuries, either in metal or in ceramic. During the reign of Louis XV, it was shaped somewhat like a weaver's shuttle, or even an oblong boat, with two lips so that the sauce could be poured out from either end. It also had two side handles and formed a single piece with its stand. Vincennes and Sèvres produced many delightful variations on the sauceboat. Under Louis XVI and later under Napoleon, the most popular models took the form of antique oil lamps, helmets, or gondolas on pedestals, with a broad pourer on one end and a handle on the other. In the nineteenth century, it was fixed on a platter to protect the tablecloth and was an integral part of the table service. Noteworthy among the many faience and porcelain sauceboat designs was the degreasing sauceboat, which had a hood on the pouring lip that made it possible to skim grease from the surface of the gravy.

The Soup Tureen

The soup tureen made its first appearance at the very start of the nineteenth century. It was larger than the *pot à oille,* but resembled it in other ways—round and deep and with its own cover—and the notch in the cover accommodating the shaft of the ladle did not come until the twentieth century. Under the Empire, great metalworkers such

1.

1. Hare paté terrine, 19th century.

2. Matching blue and white soup tureen, vegetable serving dish, and sauceboat.

as Odiot invented sumptuous tureens in the antique style, shaped like urns on pedestals and decorated with long-necked swans. After the Restoration, they assumed the round, bell-mouthed look we associate with them today; their covers had pinecones, artichokes, or tomatoes for knobs, and their handles were hollow. They often came in pairs, were part of a complete service, and existed in several sizes: for two, four, six, eight, ten, twelve, fifteen, or twenty-four people. They were made of silver or silver plate by leading nineteenth-century silversmiths like Hugo, Cardeihac, Lebrun, Ravinet d'Enfert, Tetard Freres, and Durand. In faience and porcelain, they were made by all the big potteries—Montereau, Creil, Sarreguemines, Lunéville, Gien, Saint-Clément, Longwy, and Quimper—which turned this comely, rotund object into a reassuring symbol of family virtues.

The Vegetable Dish

Smaller than the tureen, the vegetable dish with its English origins is sometimes confused with the porringer; it is round with two side handles and a cover lifted by a knob in the shape of a pinecone or a vegetable. The term first surfaced in the nineteenth century, but the object itself came into use much earlier in the 1730s and was often produced in matching pairs. When made of metal, it was sometimes accompanied by a hot plate.

The nineteenth century saw the birth of another kind of vegetable dish, which was rectangular with a cover that had a removable knob. If you took off this knob the cover could be turned over to make a second dish.

Earthenware and porcelain vegetable dishes reproduced on a smaller scale the shapes and patterns of the ordinary soup tureen. Among the most sought after are those with pinecone or garden vegetable patterns such as artichokes and carrots.

Le ravier ("Hors d'oeuvre Dishes")

The French word *ravier* probably derives from *rave*, meaning a member of the radish family. The *ravier* appeared on French tables in the 1830s as a dish for hors d'oeuvres. It was also called an *hors d'oeuvrier* or a *bateau à raves* ("radish boat") when it was longer and turned up at either end. Made in porcelain, faience, glass, crystal, and metal, it might be rectangular, oblong, or hexagonal in shape. It also came as several movable cups that formed compartments and were placed in a stand with a central handle or knob of nickel-plated copper or silver plate.

The Salad Bowl

The handle-less salad bowl has been a fixture since the seventeenth century. It was confined to the kitchen for most of its life and was only promoted to the dining table fairly recently, becoming an integral feature of table services in the late nineteenth century. Salad bowls were generally made of stoneware or porcelain and were originally much less common than the *pot à oille* or the terrine. Sometimes it was made of cut crystal, porcelain, or faience and was also sold on its own not only for serving salads but also fruits and side dishes.

TIPS FOR COLLECTORS

Soup tureens are abundant on the market and relatively cheap. It is always wiser to buy a tureen with the rest of its service than on its own. But you can still fall in love with a certain type of tureen knowing that it won't cost an arm and a leg.

A tureen is just as useful for serving vegetables or stews as it is for serving soup. Before making the purchase, make sure that the piece has no nicks or cracks in it; if the cover is missing, it may be used as a planter.

1.

2.

3.

1 to 3. All of these silver-plated models of serving dishes are copies of past styles: rectangular and oval, with cover (1.), vegetable casseroles by Christofle (2.), and soup tureens by Christofle (3.).

4. Soup tureen with refined rose design and a vegetable knob on the lid. German, early 19th century.

2.

3.

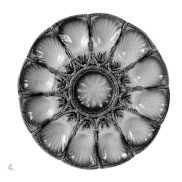

4.

Asparagus Plates, Artichoke Plates, Shellfish Plates

Once again, barbotine is king in this department, with its compartmented dishes, vegetables in relief, and fantastical shellfish. These make the brightest, most springlike table settings in the world.

For Asparagus and Artichokes

Asparagus and artichokes have been consumed in Europe since the seventeenth century, but it was not until the close of the nineteenth century that specific services were devised for them. All the leading barbotine makers seem to have produced enormous quantities of asparagus dishes. Did people eat more asparagus then than they do today? Perhaps, but it is certain that the techniques of the period for molding paste in relief made it easy to make compartmental dishes.

The asparagus service quickly won a place in the middle-class households. As a rule, it took the form of a dozen plates and a dish or two—one for serving, the other for clearing away—and a sauceboat. The plates would be decorated with a few asparagus shoots in relief or with artichoke leaves forming a separation between the space reserved for the vegetable and that for the sauce, and laid against a background of basketwork or a bed of foliage. The asparagus shoots were presented to the diners in a "cradle," usually made up of

a hollow bunch of asparagus on an oval or rectangular serving plate, sometimes as an integral part and sometimes not. Even great faience manufacturers produced their own version of these services, the most refined being those of Salins, Saint-Amand-les-Eaux, Longchamp, Lunéville, Orchies, and Sarreguemines.

Silver-plated asparagus dishes are also available, but they have none of the charm of barbotine, which goes so well with vegetable dishes and fruit.

Oyster Plates, Shellfish Plates, and Snail Plates

Equally amusing, but perhaps less varied, are barbotine oyster plates. They are nearly always round, hollow receptacles in the shape of *belon* or Portuguese oysters. In general there are six of these containers (though sometimes they run to twelve) with a seventh in the center for the lemon. Most of these plates are green in color, similar to the oysters themselves. But some manufacturers took liberties with reality and used white, gray, or pink tints.

1. A double asparagus cradle with a handle, resting on an imitation basket-weave earthenware dish.

2. A highly original asparagus dish, with two compartments, late 19th century.

3. A more classic pattern of asparagus dish. Manufacture de Sarreguemines, circa 1900.

4. Dish for a dozen oysters, with colored glaze. Manufacture de Sarreguemines, circa 1880.

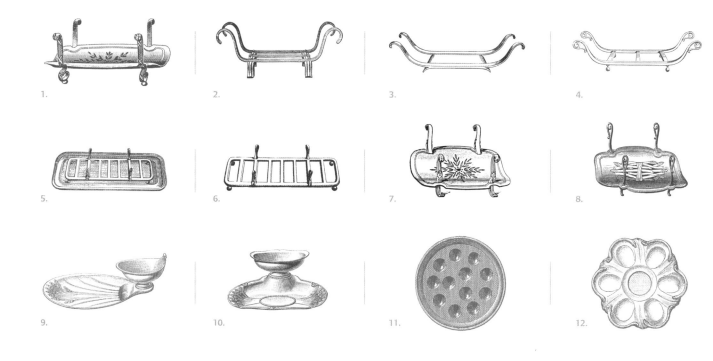

1. 2. 3. 4.

5. 6. 7. 8.

9. 10. 11. 12.

TIPS FOR COLLECTORS

Asparagus and artichoke plates take up a lot of room and are seldom used, but they have real charm. When you take interest in such things, you'll find that they come in many varieties, with more or less delicate colors and craftsmanship that ranges from crude to highly accomplished. This explains why some are more sought after than others, Choisy-le-Roi is a case in point.

Complete services are rare; the sauceboat or the detachable strainer is frequently missing. On the other hand, the plates themselves are still readily available, especially in small series.

Always favor unblemished and unchipped pieces, especially if you expect to use them at the table.

1 to 8. Asparagus cradles.

9 and 10. Asparagus dishes.

11. Snail dish, with silver interior.

12. Silver oyster dish.

13. Oyster plates with basket-weave relief.

14. The same oyster plates, in a single color.

13.

2.

Serving Eggs, Butter, and Cheese

Why not resurrect those peculiar objects known as egg carriers, eggcups, and butter dishes? Sunday brunch, for example, which is becoming a more and more popular custom, lends itself perfectly to their use.

The Presentation of Eggs

The egg stand, used for hard-boiled eggs, is made of small horizontal shelves of wood set around an upright post, with round holes for the eggs to stand in (today you can see many variations on this basic design on the counters of French cafés). The egg tray has a dozen holes for hard-boiled eggs and two small compartments for salt and pepper. The individual egg plate, usually made of earthenware, comes with eggcups, egg spoon, salt cellar, and candlestick. The egg ramekin takes the form of a small earthenware or porcelain pan with a cover and a lathe-turned wooden handle. Taking their cue from the English, the French adopted egg trays or egg services made of silver or silver plate with feet, a central handle, circlets able to hold four or six eggcups, and racks for the spoons. When they contained only two eggcups, they were known as *tete-à-tetes*.

Eggcups

The boiled egg was formerly considered a sovereign food for pregnant women and convalescents. Louis XV was the first to elevate it to the level of a dinner course. The king ate one egg every Sunday, out of a golden eggcup nestled in its own gold basket. Madame de Pompadour owned a similar model in silver. Among other celebrated eggcups were those of the Dauphin, in sky blue Sèvres porcelain, and of Marie-Antoinette, who had a blue glass egg goblet set in a silver stand.

The first eggcups were made of precious metals, gold, or silver—or both, with the exterior of silver and the interior of gold. They were given as gifts to babies at their birth or christening and to couples on their engagement; they were accompanied by a drinking cup, a spoon, and a small dish. Each would be engraved with the recipients' monogram or adorned with hearts, birds, or flower patterns. Later came small masterpieces of faience and soft-paste porcelain, and in the nineteenth century the range of materials broadened to include vermeil, opaline, crystal, and barbotine and the pieces incorporated a whole array of nests, chickens and eggshells, paste glass, and pressed glass. The French phrase *"gagner le cocotier,"* meaning "to win the coconut palm" is, interestingly enough, a deformation of *"gagner le coquetier,"* meaning "to win the eggcup." At nineteenth-century fairgrounds, a common prize at shooting stands were pressed glass eggcups.

At the end of the nineteenth century, lavishly decorated silver plate was all the rage, with its fillets, gadroons, engravings,

3.

4.

5.

1. Egg stand, made of wire, late 19th century.

2. Silver eggcups of various designs. Some of these might have had gold interiors—which increased their purchase price by 2 francs in Christofle's 1913 catalogue.

3. Egg plate.

4. *Cocotte* for boiling six eggs. There was a larger model that could hold a dozen eggs.

5. Egg tray.

1 and 2. Cylindrical butter dishes.

3. Camembert dish.

4 to 6. Covered "churns" for butter or grated cheese.

7. Silver eggcup, 1950s .

8. *Diabolo* faience and porcelain eggcups.

9. Stylized flower-patterned faience eggcup.

10. Silver butter mold for making butter "shells."

1.

2.

3.

4.

5.

6.

grooves, ribs, friezes, and traceries. Patterns proliferated, and all manner of fantasy was indulged. Many eggcups were made of wood, especially box, olive, fruit-wood, pine, and ash; exotic essences like ebony, sandalwood, and ironwood were also popular. They could be finely turned on a lathe or roughly sculpted, painted, lacquered, or pokerworked. Other materials appeared; eggcups went rustic, with stoneware and glazed earthenware, and then were reduced to their simplest form with aluminium, wire, enameled iron, and pewter. At the top end of the range, they were fashioned out of brass, horn, ivory, and finally of resolutely modern Bakelite.

Shapes

The basic shape of the eggcup always stays the same even though variations on the theme are infinite. Because it is such a small item, it is an ideal collector's item, on the condition that the collector adheres to a precise theme, ornamentation, or material.

The eggcup, which is seldom more than 4 inches in height, can be *á baluster*, meaning raised on a slightly rounded pedestal. It may also be a tripod, resting on simple balls or animal feet. The type known to the French as *demi-anglais* ("half English") has a short foot; the model known to the English as a "bucket" eggcup has no foot at all; and the *diabolo* or *bobine* is made up of two cones meeting at their narrow ends. Some eggcups come with a saucer on which the spoon can be laid and occasionally have their own built-in receptacles for salt and pepper.

Cheese Platters and Butter Dishes

Cheese was seldom consumed in the eighteenth century, though some—such as Brie—were included in favorite recipes. Fresh cheeses would be served as side dishes in charming *fromagers* (china drainers). These were cylindrical pots with holes for draining the whey into a dish fitted for the purpose.

The practice of eating cheese at the end of a meal dates from the nineteenth century, when cut-crystal or ceramic platters with matching covers emerged.

The butter dish or butter pot, on the other hand, dates back to at least the fourteenth century in Europe. It may take the form of a churn or tub with two vertical tenons placed on a fitted platter; a small dish with small cover; or a crystal container placed on a metal saucer with a metal lid that may or may not swing open and shut on a pivot. The butter cooler is usually made of porcelain or porous clay, with a glass receptacle inside; cold water in the cooler keeps the butter at the right temperature. Finally, there is the two-piece butter mold; one part is perforated, and the other fits into it. The butter, when squeezed between the two, comes out in decorative petals.

TIPS FOR COLLECTORS

The eggcup is an ideal collector's item; it takes up very little space, includes every theme under the sun, and comes in every material from barbotine and boxwood to decorated glass.

The most expensive eggcups are made of silver; style and refinement are the main elements making for value, along with the hallmarks of well-known silversmiths.

For porcelain and faience eggcups, look for well-executed design, pristine condition, and signature. Eggcups made from rare wood essences are much sought after.

Finally, look for originality in the pattern. Eggcups were often sold in sets of six to twelve and can be reconstituted one by one with patient buying.

7.

8.

9.

10.

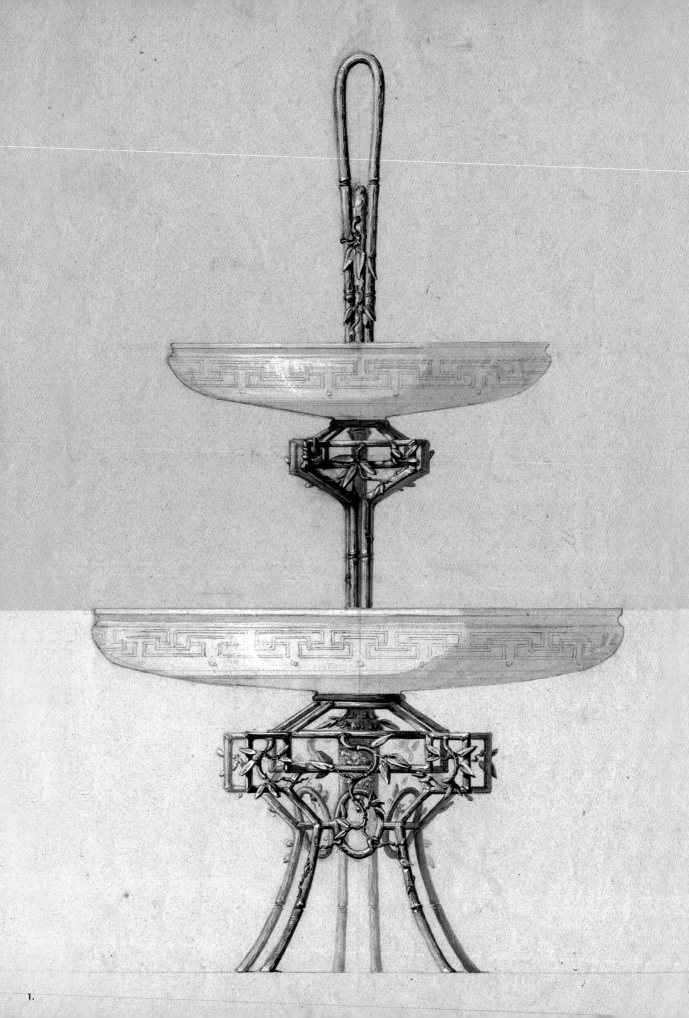

2.

3.

4.

Dessert Platters

"Dessert services are often made of cut glass, but silver and ver-meil bowls are still highly coveted, and porcelain ones never go out of fashion," declares an early-twentieth-century guide to good living. At that time, people ate more sweets and puddings in general than we do today, and this practice was all for the good, since it led to the invention of all sorts of charming plates and dishes. It would seem that, in the past, fruit and cakes were often present on the table as decoration from the very start of the meal. For this reason, fruit dishes and fruit stands, which effectively functioned as grace-ful, tall centerpieces, were produced in twos and fours.

The Compotes

The compote was used for stewed fruit (or compote) and also for fresh whole fruit, biscuits, creams, and side dishes. It had its own distinctive shape and outline: it had no wing or raised rim, but was relatively deep, so that it looked like a kind of basin with crenellated edges. When it had no feet, it could be triangular, square, rectan-gular, gondola- or shell-shaped, as exem-plified by the compotes produced by the soft-paste potteries of Saint-Cloud and Sèvres. In the nineteenth century, the compote became taller with its own stand or pedestal of varying height. It resem-bled a goblet of blown glass, cut glass, faience, silver plate, bronze, or white metal. Often it was a part of a table serv-

ice proper, in which case it would be monogrammed or emblazoned. The highly decorated, deeply cut crystal bowl with removable silver feet was especially popu-lar at the end of the nineteenth century and often formed part of the centerpiece.

Fruit Baskets

As the nineteenth century progressed, it became more and more common for fruits and cakes to be presented in "baskets" that evoked their rustic origin. The earliest were made of porcelain, but between 1850 and 1880 they began to be manufactured in vermeil, gilded bronze, or silver-plated bronze. Sometimes the metal would be woven in imitation of basketry. After 1890, wickerwork made its appearance on tables.

5.

1. Sketch of *Bambou* pattern, a tripod with two suspended crystal dishes engraved with a Greek motif. Christofle archives, circa 1860.

2 and 4. Designs for double-octagonal cake dishes: rosette pattern (left) and radiating pattern (right), as described in the contemporary Christofle catalogue.

3. Strawberry service comprising of metal frame, two dishes, sugar bowl, and creamer.

5. Reissue of a woven faience Provencal fruit basket.

1. Built-in ice buckets, for keeping ice cream and sorbets cool, made of silver plate and crystal. Christofle.

2. English stoneware preserve dish and plates. Wedgwood, 1930s.

1.

Among other curiosities in the same line were the grape basket, an oval basket made of metal or withy, with a tall handle and hooks for hanging bunches of fruit; and the chestnut dish, made of porcelain or silver, with a lid imitating a folded-back, half-open table napkin. There was also the *marronière*, a kind of openwork porcelain basket for chestnuts.

Strawberry Dishes

Strawberries were highly appreciated in the nineteenth century, and nothing was too good for them when it came to dishes and bowls. "A store in Paris (Christofle) has just launched a new strawberry basket made of silver and crystal. This basket stands in the middle of a group that forms a centerpiece. All around are crystal vessels mounted in silver that serve to contain powdered sugar, kirsch, rum, maraschino, whipped cream, and slices of orange and pineapple, which diners can add to the strawberries to taste." When strawberries were served in quantity, they were simply laid in a bowl or in crystal set in a broad woven silver basket, where they would not be bruised. Other strawberry services consisted of two fruit bowls, a creamer, and a sugar bowl, which all fit into a single base. Charming pieces of the same kind were made in faience or barbotine, with incorporated strainers.

Ice Buckets and Coolers

In the eighteenth century, there was a craze in France for sorbets and ice creams. To satisfy this trend, a new category of dish was invented: the ice bucket or cooler. It was made up of three sections, which worked in a simple, ingenious way. The first part, on the bottom, was a two-

handled bowl; a second bowl fit inside the first bowl; and over both bowls sat a concave, basin-shaped lid. The ice, which was taken from frozen ponds during the winter and stored in icehouses, was placed between the two bowls and in the hollow of the lid, and thus the sorbet and the ice cream could be kept cold. This system was perfected by Sèvres and imitated by the other soft-paste porcelain producers, before being manufactured in hard-paste porcelain. All in all, it was a magnificent, highly sophisticated object.

The craze for ices continued into the nineteenth century. People consumed them in the evening, as desserts, or after dinner in the salon, served in small individual china cups, each with its own cover, and presented on a matching tray.

Cake and Pie Platters

Porcelain makers invented a small, attractive platter with two side handles especially for cakes, with finely worked *ajouré* or lacework edges. In general, it was part of what was known as an "individual" service. The tart dish or pie platter, by contrast, was a flat item resembling the base of an actual tart, mounted on feet or on a pedestal.

TIPS FOR COLLECTORS

Nowadays, a fine, white cake platter in excellent condition, with a gold or otherwise delicately painted rim, can be purchased inexpensively.

Small ice cream pots on their matching trays, which are no longer much used, are nonetheless charming in their own fashion and have become purely decorative items.

FLATWARE

Knife, fork, and spoon: these three essential tools took many
centuries to reach the table, but once they did, they were there
to stay. In the second half of the nineteenth century, with the
invention of the silver plate, individual settings became the
norm—which prompted Chatillon-Duplessis to write in the
magazine **Salle à Manger** that "sooner or later somebody will
invent an instrument for holding your fork for you." Thereafter,
every different kind of dish had its own specific utensil.

Even though some of the flatware have ceased to exist—
such as those peculiar forks with one outer edge for cutting,
used for eating melons, fish, or cakes—their profusion is no
cause for complaint. Some of the pieces invented in the
nineteenth century are real jewels of their type, with which
the goldsmiths and silversmiths of that prolific time raised
the art of the table to unimaginable heights.

On the other hand, old silver—which had its heyday in
the eighteenth century—remains a rarity because so much
of it was melted down at one time or another by official order;
and its price today reflects this fact. But a vast selection of
flatware became available in the nineteenth century; patient
and dedicated collectors will have little difficulty in finding
whatever they are looking for at bargain prices.

Silverware

The art of the silversmith and goldsmith is among the oldest craft known to man. However, it was not until the discovery of the New World and its silver mines that the greatest European craftsmen were able to give free rein to their talents, as the rituals of the table began to require more numerous, varied, and sophisticated flatware and utensils. In the nineteenth century, silver plate began to replace sterling silver, further broadening the scope of table silver.

Old Silver

What we know as "old silver" really took off in the late seventeenth and eighteenth centuries, with great craftsmen such as Nicolas Delaunay, Claude II Balin, and Nicolas Bernier. Unfortunately, much of their work was melted down to finance the wars of Louis XIV in 1689 and 1709. For this reason, the future generation was robbed of many masterpieces of the French silver-smiths, though a few great items commissioned by foreign monarchs and aristocrats were preserved. Nevertheless, you only have to compare the scarcity of French silver with the abundance of English silver of the same era to understand to what point the former was laid waste. Apart from the sprinkling of prestige objects, only everyday objects like sugar and salt shakers, candlesticks, dishes with the corners cut off, goblets, porringers, and coffeepots remain.

The rococo style emerged around 1723, under the influence of Juste Aurele Meissonnier, who introduced the concepts of asymmetry and movement into orna-mentation. In diluted form, this style made its way into the ordinary tableware of the time, which is still appreciated and manufactured today: dishes with cham-fered rims, balustered teapots and cof-feepots, tulip-shaped cups, sugar bowls, salt cellars, candlesticks, and flatware with patterns of violins and seashells.

The silverware of the reign of Louis XVI saw a reaction to all this exuberance and then a return to the classicism of antiquity, sparked by the discovery of the ruins of Pompeii. Jacques-Nicolas Roettiers created a number of neoclassical masterpieces at this time, most notably for the Russian court.

Modern Silverware

The craft of the silversmith, which was all but lost during the Revolution, was reborn during the *Directoire* era and the Empire. Henri Auguste, Martin Guillaume Biennais, and Jean-Baptiste Claude Odiot were the masters of the time, creating monumental pieces covered in motifs in bas-relief and decorated with foliated scrolls, eagles, swans, and sphinxes, as Egypt became all the rage. The Louis-Philippe style, which accompanied the rise of a new middle class in France, coincided with the introduction of the new "head of Minerva" system of silver hallmarking. This nineteenth-century silverware has survived in abundance, seal-ing our abiding preference for the Louis XV rocaille style and the ribbons and gadroons of Louis XVI. While Froment-Meurice sup-plied the formal silverware of Napoleon III, the second half of the century was marked by a stylistic eclecticism that was charac-terized by elaborate Gothic, rococo, and Pompeian ornamentation.

The Revolution of Silver Plate

The greatest novelty of the nineteenth century was the introduction of silver plating by galvanoplasty, or electrodispo-sition. Starting in 1844, Charles Christofle began using a process invented in England

2.

Preceding pages:
Left: Silver spoons and ivory-handled, steel-bladed knives, 19th century.
Right: Louis XIV-style flatware.

1. Sterling silver vegetable dish, 18th century.

2. Sheffield silver egg tray and eggcups, 1840.

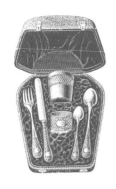

1.

2.

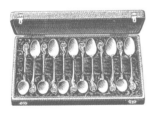

3.

4.

5.

by Elkington, which made it possible to cover a base metal with an outer layer of silver by electroplating. His products were highly successful, both among the bourgeois class, who wished to compete with and imitate the aristocracy, and among the aristocrats themselves, who were concerned about maintaining their prestige. Even the imperial family now found itself able to indulge its taste for pomp and luxury without going to excessive expense. Other gifted manufacturers followed where Christofle led; Boulenger, Ercuis, Armand-Calliat, and Poussielgue-Rusand. This period also marked the beginnings of low-cost mass production of silver plate on an industrial scale.

Toward the end of the century, ornamentation—often with vegetable motifs—became very popular, heralding the arrival of the Japanese style, naturalism, and art nouveau. Finally the 1925 style of Jean Puiforcat engendered new shapes that were much cleaner and more austere (see page 87).

Evaluating Silverware

The French word *orfévrerie* originally designated silversmiths' and goldsmiths' work. Later it was broadened to include the working of other metals and alloys including copper, brass, and nickel, which were plated with gold or silver. Thus the world "silverware" came to include the whole gamut of objects covered in silver plate.

A number of considerations come into play when you are estimating the value of a piece of silver, notably its specification, weight, crafting, and style. But the best indication of worth remains the hallmark, which gives the date, origin, and maker of the piece.

Specification

Gold and silver cannot be used pure for making utensils because they are too malleable and soft. What is known as "sterling silver" is actually a blend of silver with some other, harder metal, usually copper. Its specification is the percentage of precious metal contained in that blend.

For sterling silverware, there are two specifications: first, 925/1000 and second, 800/1000.

Hallmarks on Old Silver

So-called "old silver" originates in the period prior to 1838, the date when the Minerva-head hallmark first made its appearance. Before 1791, silverware had to carry four silver marks by law. These were:
• The master's mark, which usually consisted of the silversmith's initials.
• The guild-mastership's mark, indicating the town guaranteeing the quality of the metal. This was a letter indicating the date, which changed each year according to the alphabet.
• The charge mark was punched in during the manufacturing process by the farmer-generals whose function was to levy the silver tax, beginning in 1672. This mark was exclusive to each farmer-general and to each of France's thirty-one circumscriptions.
• The discharge mark, which proved that the tax had been duly paid and frequently took the form of an emblem—such as insect, flower, and ear.

After the Revolution, from 1798 to 1838, only three hallmarks were required:
• The master's or craftsman's mark.
• The guarantee mark, which was a rooster with its head turned to the left (pre-1809) and to the right (between 1809 and 1819). Between 1819 and 1838, the rooster was replaced by the head of an old man.
• The specification mark.

Modern Hallmarks

After 1838, so-called "modern" silver was bound by law to carry a charge mark, to which the manufacturer's mark would often be added. The charge mark remained a head of Minerva turned to the right until 1973, and thereafter turned to the left. This was accompanied by a letter of the alphabet that changed every ten years.

Silver Plate Hallmarks

Silver made in 1861 and after carries the maker's hallmark, which may be square or rectangular. After 1983, this mark became square only and came with a number indicating the quality of the silvering along with the maker's symbol and initials.

Flatware may have one of two silver plating qualities (the minimum average thickness of the silver plating, in microns). Number One quality is 33 microns, and Number Two quality is 20 microns.

For decorative pieces, the norm is 10 microns for Number One quality and 6 microns for Number Two quality.

Sheffield Plate

Invented in 1742 by Thomas Boulsover, Sheffield plate is named after the Yorkshire town that was England's main center for silverware manufacture outside London and was made using the first process to make silverware out of anything but solid silver. It consisted in taking a sheet of copper and fusing molten silver to both sides and was very successful in both England and France until the invention of silver plating by galvanoplasty (or electrodisposition) in 1840.

Incised, Engraved, and Pierced

Incising consists of beating metal with a hammer or chasing tool to create patterns or matte backgrounds.

A *repoussé* or "chased" effect is obtained when the silversmith, working on the underside of his piece, hammers areas outward to create relief.

Engraving is done by working up a design with a chisel or other etching tool.

Gadrooning is a type of concave or convex decoration, oval in form and slightly elongated.

Piercing is a technique based on contrasts between bulges and hollows.

Vermeil, Inlaid Enamelwork, and Enamelwork

Vermeil is the effect of a layer of gold on silver.

Niello, or inlaid enamelwork, consists of working a mixture of sulphur, lead, silver, or copper into the etching of a piece, which is then fired to produce a decoration of black against silver.

Enamel is made up of an opaque or transparent glass paste, in powder form, which is applied to a silver background before being fired in a kiln where it solidifies. When it is held in by soldered partitions, enamel is known as cloisonne as opposed to champlevé, where the paste is cradled in small hollows or indentations in the surface of the metal.

TIPS FOR COLLECTORS

Strasbourg, Bordeaux, Lille, Paris, and Arras are all excellent marks for old silver, but beware of counterfeits: old silver marks are sometimes soldered to new pieces. It is always a good idea to check the date offered by the silver mark against the crafting and style of a piece, verifying the placement of the silver mark and its condition.

The presence of a coat of arms increases the value of the flatware, while a monogram has the reverse effect.

In general, the older the piece, the more prized it is.

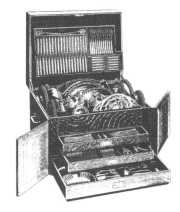

6.

1. Silver box for individual napkin ring, flatware, and cup.

2. Silver box for dessert knife, flatware, and napkin ring.

3. Silver box for strawberry spoon and sugar spoon.

4. Box of teaspoons.

5. Box for fish service knife and fork.

6. Oak silver-chest, complete with drawers, lockers, and an interior lined with chamois leather.

7. Silver restaurant vegetable dish with cover.

7.

2.

Silverware from the 1930s

The silverware from the 1930s was way ahead of its time, resolutely rejecting the overloaded style of the nineteenth century and offering instead a brand new, unsullied modernity. It is much sought after today by collectors of fine tableware, who match it with contemporary china and earthenware.

The Art of Simplification

The Paris Decorative Arts Exhibition of 1925 saw the emergence of art deco, in reaction to the undulating outlines, invasive decoration and naturalistic style of art nouveau. Its guiding principle was a return to geometric rigor and pure lines completely innocent of superfluous ornamentation.

Jean Puiforcat (1897–1945) was a key figure among the creative talents of the period. The heir to a dynasty of silversmiths and a great admirer of Maillol, Puiforcat was a sculptor and mathematician who worked in his father's workshop before studying with the sculptor Lejeune. He planned his designs on paper, creating a wide range of pieces and a score of different silver patterns using geometric shapes as his starting point: spheres, cones, cylinders, and cubes. He made things simpler, endowing the fork with its former three prongs instead of four, giving a perfect oval shape to spoons, producing knives whose blades and handles were exactly the same width, and reintro-

ducing ivory, lapis lazuli, rock crystals, shagreen, and stone for handles. Other great silversmiths followed in Puiforcat's footsteps, notably the Maison Tétard, with Valery Bizouard and Jean Tétard, Aucoc, Hénin, Boulenger, Saglier, Laparra, Boin-Taburet, Cardeilhac, and Ravinet d'Enfert. Christofle, meanwhile, turned to great modernist innovators like André Groult, Luc Lanel and Louis Sue, or the Dane Christian Fjerdingstad.

TIPS FOR COLLECTORS

One thing to keep in mind is that second-hand knives, forks, and spoons sell at roughly a third of the price of the same patterns that are brand new, and serving utensils are a quarter of the price.

While solid silver art deco table settings by a famous maker can be as expensive as eighteenth-century pieces, geometric pieces can still be purchased today at bargain prices.

3.

Individual Flatware

In the seventeenth century, guests brought their own knives and forks to a meal, for the most part snugly nestled in a finely decorated pouch. The reign of Louis XIV saw the first flatware as we know them today. The three components—knife, fork, and spoon—were all laid on one side of the plate; they were made of silver or vermeil, and gold was the king's prerogative.

The Spoon

The spoon is of great antiquity, its oval shape being borrowed from the form of a cupped hand. It began as a simple piece of carved wood. During the Middle Ages, its bowl became more rounded, the handle was as broad as the end, and it was held in a fist. During this time, it was made of wood or pewter.

The fashion for elaborate lace ruffs and collars, which were easily ruined by spillage, logically inspired a longer, flatter handle toward the end of the sixteenth century. In the seventeenth century, the spoon became a refined, valuable object with an intricately carved handle, and by the end of the century, smaller specialized spoons had begun to appear for the new beverages of tea and coffee and for side dishes such as strawberries or boiled eggs. These spoons came in bone, ivory, or horn.

The Fork

The fork came into use in Italy during the fifteenth century, reaching France with Catherine de Medicis and the court of her son, Henri III. At this time it had only two prongs and was still short and rustic in appearance, with a thick stem and sharp angles. It would be shared by several people at once, a practice that came to be deemed unhygienic and dismissed by the French aristocracy. After 1640, it acquired a third prong and a stem ending in a dovetail, the precursor of the flat fork; the end of its spatula became trilobed (split into three lobes). Meanwhile Louis XIV continued to eat with his fingers. Around 1680, the fork was given a fourth prong, and its

spatula became distinct from its stem; but still it was used by only a few. Even Louis XVI spurned it, preferring to skewer his food with the point of his knife. Forks only became the norm at meals at the end of the eighteenth century.

The Knife

In the Middle Ages, knives with pointed blades were generally used to pierce food and carry it to the mouth. During the Renaissance, the knife went beyond this purely utilitarian function to become a symbol of prestige: it would be made of gold or silver, with handles of ivory, mother-of-pearl and precious or semi-precious stones—which were popularly believed to give protection against poison. At the time everyone carried his own, usually folding, knife in a fine pouch at his belt. The handle would be of ivory finely carved with scenes from hunting or mythology, or with images of fantastic creatures when they were not made of hand-decorated faience. The blades were exquisitely etched and made of gold, silver, or steel. The main centers for knife manufacture in the seventeenth century were Paris, Strasbourg, and eventually Langres.

Under Louis XIV, knives began to be made with silver handles; silver was a malleable metal that allowed the smiths to make invisible solderings and devise more delicate decorations. Sadly, many of these pieces were melted down by official order of the French government to finance its wars and were quickly replaced by knives with faience, china, or rock crystal handles. Later, Cardinal Richelieu passed an

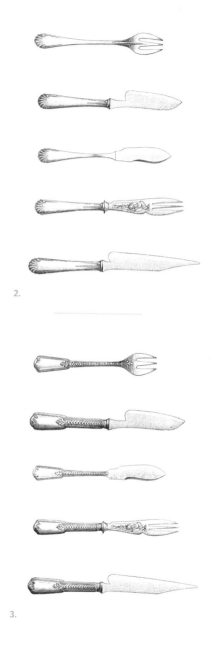

2.

3.

1. Silver-plated flatware, 19th century and 1930s.

2 and 3. From the top: oyster fork, cheese knife, butter knife, cutting-edge melon fork, and melon knife. This Christofle flatware are in the *Directoire* style (2.) and Louis XIV style (3.).

edict that made round-ended knives compulsory; it was said that he found Chancellor Séguier's habit of picking his teeth with the point of his knife thoroughly disagreeable. In the eighteenth century, the trend was for knives to have silver blades and filled handles of ebony or mother-of-pearl. At this time the blade began to have a prolongation (the "fang"), which was fixed into the handle.

In the nineteenth century, individual table knives became part of the household's cutlery cabinet, where—side by side with the fork and spoon—they formed the nucleus of the standard flatware or individual place setting. After 1850, the forging, stamping, laminating, and polishing of knife blades became mechanical and the creating of their handles became automated.

Proliferating Patterns

The second half of the nineteenth century saw the invention of silver plate and the mass production of new individual flatware. At this time, some manufacturers opted to make sets of knives that were no longer part of the service and harked back to the Renaissance and the Middle Ages with handles of ebony, ivory, or horn.

Special knives and forks for fish appeared at the close of the century; an interesting variant on these was the single fish knife-cum-fork—a fork with a cutting edge on one of its outside prongs. Prior to the First World War, the blades of fish knives, which like the forks that went with them, were traditionally made of silver plate and engraved with motifs inspired by nature; afterward, in the 1930s, there was a return to sobriety and the absence of ornamentation.

Silversmiths were freely inspired by the shapes of crustaceans and mollusks. The oyster fork, for example, quickly became a classic. Snails had their grips and their two-pronged forks, winkles their mini-forks, and lobsters their tongs and

scoops; even the consumption of crayfish required a specific utensil. Prawns had to be stripped of their armor "with a knife and fork—a complicated undertaking indeed," as a guide to good living noted in the early twentieth century.

Curiosities

A number of unusual items appeared on tables in the late nineteenth and early twentieth centuries. These included the marrow spoon, a kind of siphon with a hollow stem that scooped marrow from beef bones; the melon fork with a cutting blade; and individual asparagus tongs, which did not last long because "they were used to carry the *entire asparagus* to the mouth, a thoroughly inconvenient exercise that was carried out clumsily at best, and which led many tables to dispense with the use of these little instrument."

For desserts and fruits, there was a whole series of individual flatware; miniature forks and spoons, two-pronged cake forks, three-pronged fruit forks, silver- or vermeil-bladed knives with mother-of-pearl, ivory, or ebony handles, melon knives, and little butter spreaders. These dessert and fruit flatware were more densely decorated than other pieces, and the blades, the backs of the forks, and the bowls of the spoons were often engraved with flowing, nature-inspired motifs.

There were all manner of specific spoons; teaspoons, coffee spoons (which the French referred to as *à la russe*), mocha spoons, soup spoons, boiled egg spoons (these were often gilded to prevent oxidation caused by the egg yolk), soda spoons, coffee glass spoons with long handles, water glass spoons with a small pestle, instead of a bowl, for crushing sugar; sauce spoons, cake spoons, syrup spoons, and cocktail swizzlers.

Cutlery Cabinets

The earliest sets of table cutlery appeared

1.

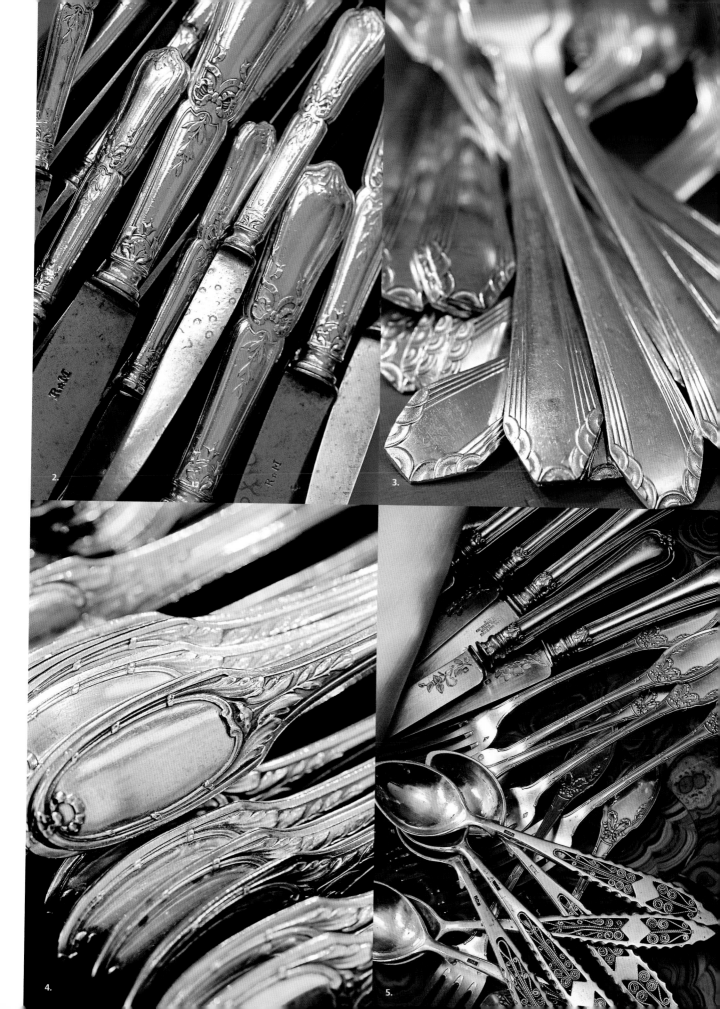

2.

3.

4.

5.

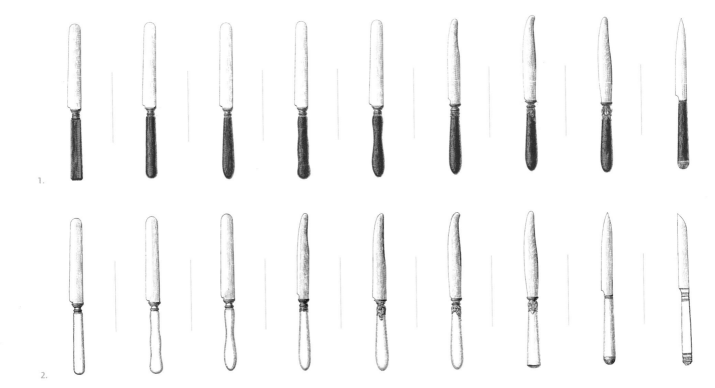

1.

2.

ETYMOLOGY

The French word **couvert** ("cover") originally meant everything that covered the table, hence the expression **mettre le couvert**, meaning "to set the table." It also means the place setting with knife, spoon, and eventually fork—three utensils that are now so familiar to us that we forget they only arrived on our tables as a team as recently as the 18th century.

1. Steel- or silver-bladed knives with ebony handles.

2. Steel- or silver-bladed knives with ivory handles.

3. Cutting-edge melon forks with ivory handles, 19th century.

4. Silver-plated flatware, various styles.

in the eighteenth century and were kept in Levantine leather boxes, small cases, or specially adapted pieces of furniture. They were small, with six or twelve of each item. Much more complete sets arrived in the nineteenth century and became common during the reigns of Louis-Philippe and Napoleon III, with 100 to 150 pieces. At this time, they also turned into one of the principal symbols of middle-class affluence and for a century thereafter they remained, along with household linen, an essential element of the marriage trousseau.

Palm Leaves and queues-de-rat Spoons

Up until 1730, the spoon design known as *queue-de-rat* ("rat's tail"), on account of a narrow reinforcing bulge running lengthwise along the outside of its bowl, was the most widespread in France. Afterward, the flat, plain, and unadorned model predominated right up to the Revolution.

Likewise, the coquille pattern, in the form of a stylized scallop, first emerged around 1700 and was quickly followed by the violon-coquille style. The scallop was sometimes enhanced by a fillet at this

time, and the first signs of a disconnecting of stem from spatula appeared

Under the Regency and in the reign of Louis XV, curves were accentuated, and ornamentation grew heavier and more asymmetrical as the rocaille style gained momentum.

The period of Louis XVI saw a return of austerity and discretion in the matter of ornament, with the arrival of simple knots, ribbons, acanthus leaves, and palm leaves.

Nineteenth-Century Fashion

Under the Empire, sobriety was the watchword and antiquity the inspiration. During Louis-Philippe's reign, there was a revisiting of earlier styles, with the return of the flat and fillet patterns and pearl and ribbon motifs. Under the influence of England, the style of Napoleon III produced an upsurge of extravagant romanticism, with heavy, over-elaborate knives, forks, and spoons in a jumble of rococo and neo-Pompeian influences. But by the end of the century, the vogue for Japan had replaced this style with a graceful, encroaching form of ornamentation, often inspired by plants and always sinuous in its lines.

1. English fruit knife and fork with Japanese decorations.

2. English fruit knife and fork, in Louis XVI style.

3. English fruit knife and fork, with "modern" handle and *Directoire* blade.

4. English silver-plated fruit knives and forks with ivory handles, 19th century.

TIPS FOR COLLECTORS

The old flat and "rat's tail" spoons are the most sought after. As a rule, complete sets of old knives, forks, and spoons are rare and expensive. The best solution therefore is to deliberately select a model and then assemble a set piece by piece.

Large spoons are more readily available than large forks.

Houses like Christofle had many different patterns to offer, which, depending on the richness of their decoration, were called **simples**, **quarts-riches** ("quarter-rich"), **demi-riches** ("half-rich"), **riches**, and **très riches**. The **simples** sets tend to be more appreciated today than the **riches and très riches**.

Take particular care to check the condition of each piece. Forks should have straight prongs, all in good condition, with no ends missing. The handles of old knives should be impeccably joined and fixed to their blades. In almost every case, it is a bad idea to restore a knife—a modicum of wear and tear is perfectly acceptable.

A good flatware is one you use. Silver and plate knives, forks, and spoons are never more beautiful than when they are fulfilling their proper function. To keep them in mint condition, store them in a case of their own: this will prevent them from rubbing against each other and protect the metal from being dulled by the light. Hunt for an old empty silver case—or failing that, have one custom-made.

Washing and storing silverware

Silver and silver plate can be put in the dishwasher if it is not mixed with items made of steel.

Knives with filled-in handles or glued collars must be washed by hand, without being left to soak; the same goes for horn, ivory, or tortoiseshell.

It is recommended that all forks, knives, and spoons be carefully dried after washing to remove any lingering stains, and then stored in a dark place. Ideally they should be placed in a silver cabinet or in pouches, but chamois leather, black tissue paper, or aluminum foil are perfectly acceptable. Avoid all contact with rubber.

Restoring knives

The best course in most cases is to find a specialist, but certain repairs can be carried out at home, if done with care.

To reglue a knife handle, scrape the inside of the handle with an old screwdriver to remove any residual wax or glue. Again using the screwdriver, refill two thirds of the cavity with epoxy glue. Then press the "fang" of the blade home, taking care that the bolster adheres well to the handle. Remove any extra glue with a piece of soft cloth, then bind the two components in place with scotch tape. Leave to dry for twenty-four hours.

To de-oxidize a steel blade, clean it with half an onion or potato, then rub with a cork or very fine sandpaper.

To straighten a knife blade, hold the blade in a vise between two pieces of hardwood and lever it straight.

To repair a nicked blade, set it in a vise and smooth out the nicks with a fine file or fine-grained whetstone. Sharpen the entire cutting edge, then polish with sandpaper.

To sharpen a steel knife blade, rub it on an oiled whetstone. Under any circumstances, do not use this method on silver-plated blades.

Straightening the prongs of a fork

If the prongs are bent against each other, straighten them with a flat wooden ruler.

If they are bent forward or backward, wrap them in a cloth and squeeze them little by little in a vise till they reach the right alignment.

Removing a bump from a spoon

If this is inside the bowl of the spoon, place it on a wooden surface and tap it gently with a round-headed hammer.

If the bump is on the outside of the spoon, make a mold with spackle or putty, then stick the mold to a wooden mount. Lay the spoon over it and tap it gently with a round-headed hammer.

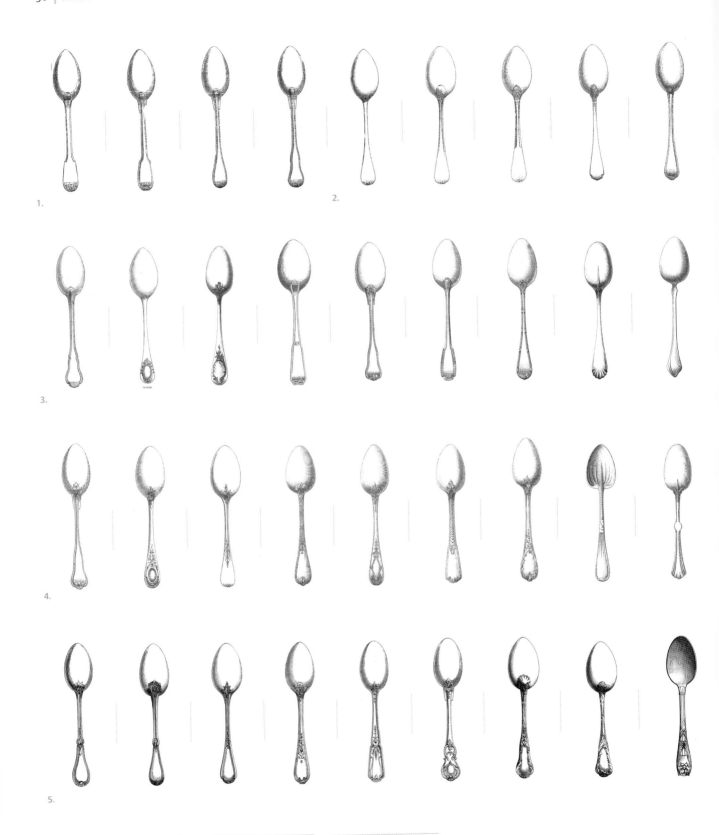

1.

2.

3.

4.

5.

1 to 5. Tea and coffee spoons by
Christofle: *Simple* series, 1891
(1.), *Quart riche* series (2.),

Demi-riche series, 1913 (3.),
Riche series, 1913 (4.), and
Très riche series, 1891 (5.).

6. Silver-plated flatware of
different styles, 19th and
20th century.

Serving Utensils

Like individual flatware, serving utensils became infinitely various in the second half of the nineteenth century. There was no dish or dessert that didn't have its own special serving tools. Was this because silversmiths were engaging in marketing strategy, creating demand where there was none before? Or was it merely because of the sheer wealth and ostentation of the period? Whatever the answer, the adaptation of forms to specific functional uses, the manifold designs, and the diversity of patterns that were created during this time continue to delight us.

Hors d'oeuvre Sets

The hors d'oeuvre set was largely an invention of the turn of the nineteenth century. It comprised of a charming series of finely wrought pieces, among them the tuna scoop, which had holes to drain the oil from the fish; the butter scoop; the olive spoon, which was often elaborately decorated; and forks designed for sausages, gherkins, sardines, and pickles (reflecting the craze for all things English), which resembled miniature tridents. Another interesting item was the small paté scoop with its rectangular spatula.

Carving Meat and Presenting Fish

The service for game also had its moment of glory at the turn of the century. The head of the household was expected to officiate with carving knife and fork while his guests looked on; roast game would be brought whole to the table for him to cut up and serve. The fork was long handled, with three silver-plated prongs; the carving knife had a steel blade and sometimes it came with a matching sharpener. When a leg of lamb was served, the fork was replaced by a handle with a clamp or screw grip, which allowed the carver to hold the joint steady with one hand. The accompanying small vegetables were threaded onto skewers and laid beside the meat; sauces and gravy were served with gravy dippers or stew spoons, which were straight, bent, round, or oval and sometimes had two pouring beaks—one for fat, the other for stock. A two-pronged fork was used for serving cold cuts.

Fish was generally served with a flat trowel with a delicately incised blade.

Serving Asparagus

In Louis XIV's reign, asparagus shoots were already being cultivated in hothouses so they could be enjoyed all year round. The nineteenth century worked out imaginative new ways of presenting this delicious vegetable. They could be moved from cradle to plate with a simple broad scoop, with flat tongs with a handle, or with a utensil similar to salad scissors with a flat crosswise grip, or with a "hand," which was essentially a pair of tongs without a handle, squeezed with the fingers.

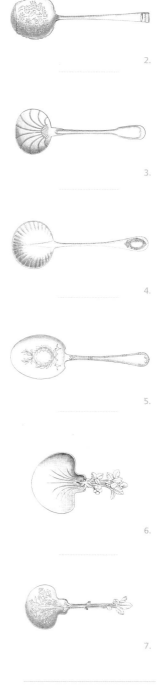

1. Sugar spoons: English, French, and perforated French, 19th century.

2 to 7. Strawberry spoons: perforated (2.), lined (3.), Louis XVI coat of arms (4.), Louis XVI crossed ribbons (5.), strawberry scoop with strawberry plant handle (6.), and sugar spoon with strawberry plant handle (7.).

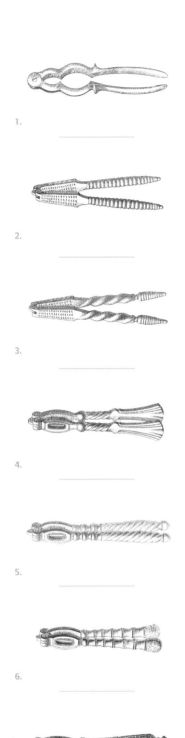

1.

2.

3.

4.

5.

6.

7.

8.

1 to 8. Nutcrackers from the 1913 Christofle catalogue.

(1.) Sprung. (2.) Gadroon. (3.) Twisted. (4.) Lotus. (5.) Twisted with bobbles. (6.) Bamboo. (7.) Facetted (8.) With knife handle.

9. Serving utensils, 19th century.

10. Bone-handled salad spoon and fork; silver-plated serving knife and fork for fish, with sleeve handles, 19th century.

Following pages:

1. Assorted silver-plated serving utensils, Louis XVI style, circa 1880 and 1930.

2. English cake scoop.

3. French strawberry scoop, 19th century.

4. French, sterling silver, perforated cake scoop, 19th century.

5. English hors d'oeuvre or pickle fork, 19th century.

Salad Forks and Spoons

The long-handled salad fork and spoon were usually made of ivory or horn, since metal oxidizes on contact with vinegar; though their handles might be of silver or plate. The patent detachable salad utensil, which allowed the host to mix the salad with two hands, and then serve it using just one hand, had only the briefest of careers.

For Eggs

The boiled egg topper came in two forms: one like scissors and the other like a spatula with a hole in it. It was accompanied, as a rule, by a pierced egg spoon. Fried or poached eggs were served with a scoop similar to an ice scoop, but round: the ice scoop was invariably oval.

For Condiments

The tiny salt spoon and the no less tiny mustard spoon have existed since the eighteenth century. Sometimes they came with a matching cylindrical nutmeg grater; they were often as carefully decorated as their much larger brethren.

Cheese and Dessert Servers

Cheese was always served with the special steel-bladed knife that we know today. The bread that came with the cheese was picked out of the bread basket with a special fork or scoop, since it was deemed ill-mannered to reach over and take a piece of bread with your fingers.

Ice creams were served with a special knife or scoop; tarts were served with a scoop; and cakes with a cake knife.

Fruit and syrup spoons, long and sinuous, are especially elegant, as are strawberry spoons whose bowls, which are often in chased silver, are designed to resemble fruits. Grapes were cut with special silver grape scissors decorated with vine leaves and grape clusters. Finally, the punch ladle had a crosswise bowl that narrowed on each side to a beak for pouring; its handle was made of wood for three quarters of its length.

Confections

Powdered sugar was sprinkled with delicate fretted scoops or with round or oval perforated spoons whose inner surfaces were gilded. Sugarloaf, crushed beforehand with a hatchet, could only be served in the English style, with sugar tongs.

Other charming items in the repertoire of confection servers are the bonbon spoon, the sugar spoon, the *petit-four* scoop, the nut spoon, and the candied fruit fork.

TIPS FOR COLLECTORS

Silver serving utensils are a pure delight. There is so much pleasure in discovering objects such as these whose uses are mostly unknown to us today.

Some of the bargains you can still find today are small sets of silver hors d'oeuvre or dessert services with mother-of-pearl handles.

Carving knives and salad forks and spoons with ebony or horn handles are also highly affordable.

9.

10.

2.

3.

4.

5.

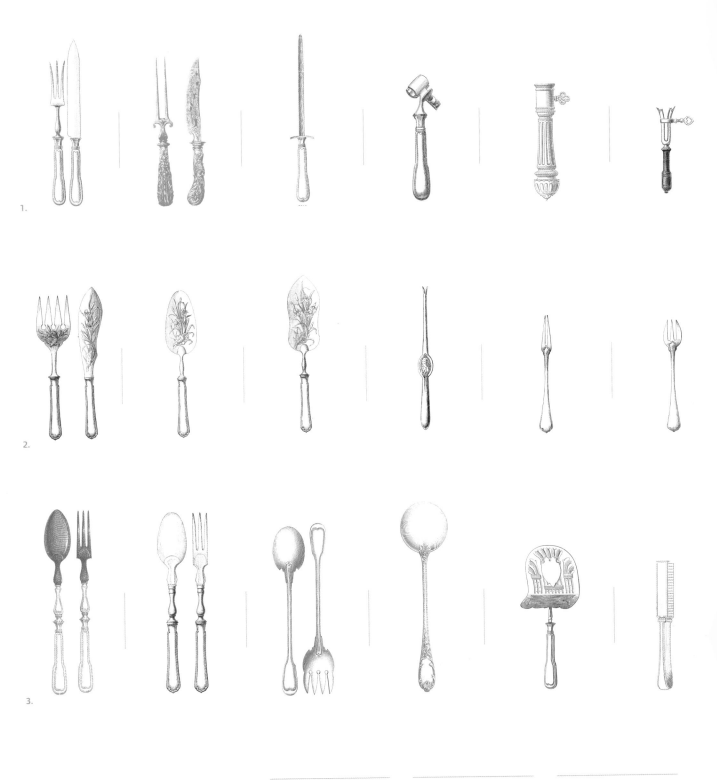

1.

2.

3.

1. Carving knife and fork,
leg-of-lamb set, sharpener,
tilting gripper, screw gripper, and
cutlet gripper.

2. Contoured fish serving knife
and fork, oval fish scoop, fish
scoop, lobster fork, snail fork,
and oyster fork.

3. Flanged salad spoon and fork,
Japanese salad spoon and fork,
English salad spoon and fork,
ladle, asparagus scoop, and
asparagus tongs.

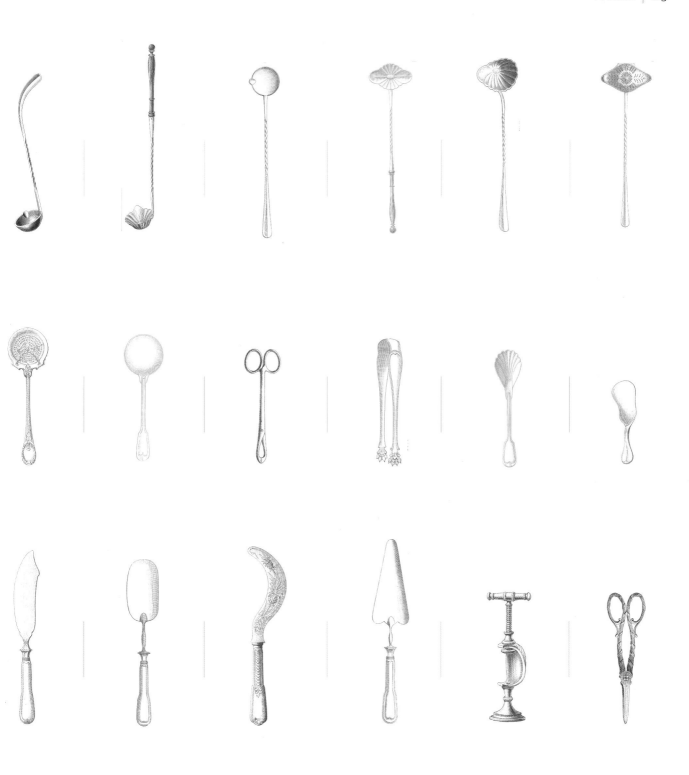

4. Fruit spoon, ribbed fruit spoon, syrup spoon, double-beaked punch ladle, single-beaked punch ladle, and Maytrank serving spoon with perforated cover.

5. Louis XVI sugar spoon, Brazilian sugar spoon, sugar cutter-tongs, shell-shaped sugar scoop, and standard sugar scoop.

6. Ice knife, ice scoop, ice hook, tart scoop, nutcracker, and Louis XV grape scissors.

All these models are Christofle originals, except the second in (1.).

Deluxe Silverware

The silver of grand hotels, ocean liners, and railroads, with its charming but functional knives and forks, robust tableware and romantic monograms, strongly evokes the early years of a leisured society engrossed in its cruises, cures, and summer resorts.

On the Trains

In the years after 1880, the railroad network in France developed very rapidly as people flocked to the seasides of Brittany, northern France, and the Riviera. Empress Eugènie had launched Biarritz as a resort, and the English came in droves to winter in Nice. The Orient Express carried its wealthy passengers across Europe to Istanbul. Train travel caught the imagination and inspired filmmakers and writers. The *Compagnie Internationale des Wagons-Lits*, founded in 1884, carried its rich clients in luxury trains where they were expected to dress impeccably for dinner in restaurant cars worthy of luxury hotels. The railroad companies of Europe also owned the station buffets, and their flatware was specially commissioned from the great silversmiths, Christofle in particular, with every piece monogrammed. (CWL, or WL, were the monograms of the *Compagnie des Wagons-Lits*). The letters would be engraved on one side or the other of the knives, forks, and spoons, depending on whether they were made for English or French trains.

In Hotels and Restaurants

All along the coast from Le Touquet to Menton, in every ski resort and spa

towns of France, luxurious palace hotels sprang up, many with casinos attached. Paris and her hotels—the Hotel du Louvre (1855), the Grand Hotel (1862), the Ritz (1898), the Crillon (1907), the Lutetia (1910), and the Claridge (1914)—attracted more and more tourists, notably when Universal Exhibitions were under way. Tens of thousands of monogrammed knives, forks, and spoons were turned out by the great silversmiths of France to equip these hotels.

On the Ocean Liners

The great shipping lines also turned to France's silversmiths, glassmakers, and porcelain manufacturers to design and produce tableware, crystal stemware, and silverware especially for them. This was the case of the liners *Ile-de-France* and *Atlantique* launched respectively in 1927 and 1930, and also of the *Normandie*, whose first crossing was made from Le Havre to New York in 1935. Puiforcat supplied the silverware for her luxury cabin suites, with an original pattern named for the ship, while Christofle furnished no fewer than forty-five thousand different pieces for the first and third class for Luc Lanel's *Transat* line. The tourist class tableware was assigned to Ercuis.

2.

1. Silver-plated restaurant duck press, with elephant heads.

2. Soup spoons, engraved "Atlantic Transport Line." England.

3. Silver-plated English dishes, utensils, and cutlery, from different hotels and restaurants.

1.

2.

TIP FOR COLLECTORS

Over the years many of the older grand hotels sold their silverware at auctions, where a collector could find plenty of bargains. This is no longer the case.

Hotel silverware was designed to withstand constant use and rough handling; it had to be very robust, and for this reason the layer of silver with which it was plated was often thicker than the legal norm.

If you are in the market for hotel flatware, you should expect them to be somewhat dented or worn.

While an anonymous monogram tends to lower the value of a piece, the initials of cruise lines such as the CGT (**Compagnie Générale Transatlantique**) will add value. The English in particular commissioned vast quantities of flatware for their yacht clubs, gentlemen's clubs, and assorted sporting associations, all of which had to have custom-made flatware.

How to clean tarnished silverware

There are all kinds of fairly straightforward techniques for cleaning silverware, which involves the use of potato peel, soot, and even powdered cuttlefish bone. Here are a few more that are equally simple and effective;

• Alcohol with a pinch of whiting works well as a cleaning agent, as does the pot liquor from boiled spinach or potatoes.

• For smaller objects, line a bowl with aluminum foil and pour in a mixture of hot water and plenty of coarse salt. Soak the objects in this solution for thirty seconds; remove and rub them vigorously.

• If the tarnishing is severe, try cleaning the piece with a solution of one part vinegar and one part ammonia. Make sure to do this in open air or in a well-ventilated room. Rinse and polish.

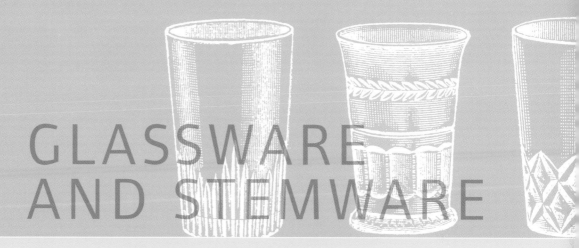

GLASSWARE
AND STEMWARE

Our grandmother's cupboards were filled with crystal glasses that were only brought out on red-letter days. It went without saying that every family had its complete service of water tumblers, glasses for red and white wine, flute glasses and coupe glasses for champagne, and liqueur glasses of various types. Some families had several sets, usually made by Baccarat or Saint-Louis, the grandest and most expensive suppliers.

Times have changed. While everyone agrees that nothing compares to a clear crystal glass with a slender stem for drinking a fine red wine, a goblet or a mug will do adequately for drinking water, and champagne flutes can vary greatly, as can white wine glasses. Nor is it the custom nowadays to have matching glasses and decanters. People buy much smaller sets of glasses so they can vary their shape or color. It has also become possible to buy crystal glasses one by one, and this has motivated collectors to assemble sets of good glasses without any particular urgency and thus without bankrupting themselves. The art of laying an elegant table is much more flexible and relaxed than it used to be, with the result that charming items such as **bistrot** glasses, absinthe glasses, beer mugs, and other assortments, which can be found in any secondhand store, have begun to appear on people's tables.

Glass or Crystal?

Italy, Bohemia, and England successively dominated the European glass trade before France finally had its turn in the nineteenth century. At this time, French craftsmen began producing the crystal glasses of unsurpassed beauty, which came to adorn not only the tables of France, but also of czars and maharajahs.

Unknown Beginnings

No one knows for sure when glass was discovered, but four thousand years ago, it was already being made in Egypt, Italy, and Syria. And it was the glassmakers of Syria, in the first century BC, who invented the extraordinary technique of glassblowing, which spread rapidly throughout the Roman Empire and beyond and is still practiced today.

The Expanding Influence of Venice

At the beginning of the eleventh century, glass kilns were established in the Veneto region of Italy and around Genoa, producing glass of remarkable quality. In the fifteenth century, Venetians invented a white glass called *cristallo*, and Venice became famous for its enamel decorations; its glass imitated malachite and onyx, and filigree glass incorporated thin glass tubes. These products were exported all over Europe and created a Venetian style that remained unchallenged until the eighteenth century.

Bohemian Glass

The glass industry that had existed in Bohemia since the eleventh century began to grow seriously in the fourteenth century. The region produced a potassium-based, transparent form of glass, which was hard, shiny, and highly refractory with qualities that favored the kind of high-relief engraving that had formerly been restricted to rock crystal. In the sixteenth century, Caspar Lehmann invented a technique for cutting and engraving glass with a disc. After 1730, Bohemian glass gained prominence over the Venetian, and by mid-

century, Bohemian glassmakers had begun cutting glass that had two or more layers of color. This type of glass flooded Europe until the Seven Year's War, the continental blockade, and the Napoleonic Wars made international commerce almost impossible.

The English Invention of Crystal

In 1615, James I of England, facing a shortage of wood in his kingdom, made it illegal for glassmakers to use it for firing their kilns. In 1676, George Ravenscroft (1618–1681), a London glassmaker who had worked in Venice, began substituting coal for wood and, in the process, also replaced potassium with lead as an ingredient. He called the result "flint glass;" crystal had been born. Thereafter the invention of heavier cutting discs made it possible to obtain decorations of extraordinary precision. Taking over from Venice and Bohemia, this crystal remained a near total English monopoly for close to a hundred years, until 1782.

French Glass

During the Middle Ages in France, most of the glassmakers were itinerant and used up immense quantities of wood. In 1615, there were no fewer than three thousand glassmakers in the kingdom. It was not until the mid-sixteenth century that glass began to be produced in fixed locations. Brushwood was the main fuel, and fern ash, mixed with potassium, formed a solid that could be shaped with tongs. From the sixteenth to the eighteenth century, this common, light, and brilliant glass, known as *verre de fougère* ("fern glass"), whose hue varied

2.

from region to region, was firmly in fashion. But toward the mid-eighteenth century, the authorities became alarmed by the increasing deforestation of the country, and the use of fern as fuel was prohibited.

In the seventeenth century, in parallel with the French production of *verre de fougère*, Italian glassmakers from the town of Altara, near Genoa, emigrated to France's Nevers region. These skillful artisans began fashioning glasses in the Venetian style, stretching the material into fillets as delicate as lace. Among these extraordinarily innovative craftsmen was Bernardo Perrotto, known in France as Bernard Perrot, who started a factory in Orleans in 1662 and invented, among many things, a translucent red glass that imitated agate and porcelain.

By the beginning of the eighteenth century, Lorraine and Normandy, as well as Nevers, Nantes, Paris, and Orleans, had become famous centers of glassmaking.

Perfecting the French Crystal

Throughout the nineteenth century, French crystal was distinguished for its purity—and for its makers' continual quest for technical advances and new levels of perfection.

Among the foremost producers was the Munzthal glassworks, created in Lorraine in 1586, which became the *Verreries Royales de Saint-Louis* in 1787. In 1781, this factory, which also specialized in windowpanes and goblets, was the first in France to produce genuine crystal and in 1825 it ceased manufacture of any other products. Saint-Louis achieved complete mastery of color, created opalines of wondrous beauty, and, among other things, invented the first *millefiori*—floral pattern meaning "thousand flowers"—ball.

Baccarat had a roughly similar experience. Founded in 1764 by the Bishop of Metz, Baccarat began by producing window glass at a hamlet of the Vosges forest some 31 miles from Nancy, then moved on to Bohemian-style glass before focusing entirely on the manufacture of crystal. With its carefully weighted composition of materials and artisans who were incom-

parably skilled at glass cutting and engraving, Baccarat became synonymous with perfection.

In the Paris region, Madame de Pompadour acquired in 1750 the privilege of the *Verrerie de Chaillot*, which she later transferred to Sèvres, where she installed the glassworks in the precincts of her chateau. Also at Sèvres was the *Manufacture des Cristaux et Èmaux de la Reine*, founded in 1784; this was subsequently moved to Moncenis, near Le Creusot, and finally closed down in 1832. Other high quality glassworks in the Paris region were Choisy-le-Roi (1821–1851), Bercy (1827–1835), and Boulogne, which became Clichy in 1844. Clichy, the third largest French producer of crystal, was absorbed by Sèvres in 1885.

At the close of the nineteenth century, art nouveau, under the influence of Emile Gallé and the Ecole de Nancy, introduced new forms that were more attuned to decorative pieces than glassware. This was the case of Daum, founded in 1870. It was not until the 1920s and René Lalique that glassware regained the same level of importance it had enjoyed in the nineteenth century.

TIPS FOR COLLECTORS

Distinguishing glass from crystal
Crystal should sound "crystalline" like a bell. It is usually more transparent than glass, heavier, and more reflective of light.

Old glasses
To identify an old glass, pass your finger under its foot. If you feel the unevenness caused by the glassmaker's pontil rod, it is old; this unevenness was smoothed off beginning in the nineteenth century.
An old glass is irregular, with imperfections, bubbles, and impurities.
The lighter the glass is, the older it is.
The foot of an old glass is often almost as wide as its lip.
Bohemian glass, cut and colored, is coming back into fashion today. The older it is, the deeper and more iridescent its colors.

1. Series of European crystal glasses, 18th and 19th century.

2. Exquisitely colored Rhine wine glasses, 18th century.

3. Lorraine crystal glasses engraved with Joan of Arc motif.

4. Champagne coupes, carafe, and Portuguese tall glasses made of colored crystal.

ETYMOLOGY

Superior crystal is a grade of glass containing at least 30% lead oxide; **crystal** contains at least 24% lead oxide; **crystalline** or **half-crystal** contains between 10% and 24%; **sonore** ("resonant") glass contains about 10%.

1.

2.

3.

4.

Bottles, Carafes, and Pitchers

Should wine be served in a decanter? In France people tend to pour really good wine from where it lives, in the bottle. But for domestic wines and cool light wines, a carafe with its fine, full shape is ideal (hence the expression *vin de carafe*). The decanter is also useful for water, but an interesting pitcher will do quite as well.

2.

Old Bottles

The French word *carafe* derives from the Arabic *gharaf*, meaning a bottle. Up until the close of the seventeenth century, bottles used for serving wine (the practice of bottling and corking them came later) were made on the spot, in the wine-producing zones. Such bottles were made of metal, faience, or blown glass, which was transparent, light green, dark green, or amber according to the region. They also had differing shapes: cylindrical, spherical with a long, ringed collar or handle, smooth sided or ribbed, with bottoms bulging inward to settle the lees. In the eighteenth century, certain bottles represented the measuring units for particular types of wine, and acquired the names of their regions: thus the *frontignan*, the *bordelaise*, or the flat Armagnac bottle inherited from the Spanish wine flask, which was generally popular until that period. Some bottles were made of black glass, invented a century earlier in England and based on coal.

Chilled wine was served at meals in the seventeenth and eighteenth centuries in preference to water, which was generally of poor quality and only used to dilute the wine. Like glasses in their racks, bottles were kept throughout the meal in coolers placed on a side table or on the floor. For many centuries, bottles were

3.

made exclusively of blown glass, which accounts for the diversity of their shapes, irregularities, and defects. In the eighteenth century, they were blown in molds, in two parts decorated with melon sides, ribs, and spirals. The decanter proper was invented in England in 1780.

The Carafe Comes to the Table

In the nineteenth century, the carafe was admitted to the table, along with the sets of individual glasses with which it was invariably matched. As a rule, each service included two models of carafe: the larger of the two was for water, the smaller for wine. In a nod to the past, some were shaped like ewers, amphoras, or helmets; others were bellied out at the bottom, or straight-sided, with or without handles and stoppers. Red wine carafes were cut, engraved, or chased in gold; Rhine wine carafes were made of simple cut crystal. Opaque or transparent, colorless or tinted, carafes were the fruit of glassmakers' boundless imaginations.

For those who insist on serving wine straight from the bottle, metal bottle carriers or panniers in plated silver and wickerwork have existed since the nineteenth century. For the rest, the decanter—with or without a handle—and the funnel are indispensable.

4.

1. Ice bowl.

2. Champagne bucket.

3. Soda-water holder with thumb grip.

4. Rhine wine bucket.

5. 19th-century, twisted glass carafe and a set of glass stoppers.

6. Beautifully wrought, cut-glass vinegar and oil cruets with silver lids, 18th century.

7. Blown glass and cider carafe, 19th century.

8. Carafe and cider or lemonade glasses, 19th century, and ribbed carafe, 18th century.

Pitchers

Pitchers are small, beaked jugs that served, first and foremost, as measures of capacity. Their thick sides helped to keep water cool. They were made of glazed terra-cotta in the countryside and of faience in the towns. Every region in France had its own type of pitcher: azure terra-cotta around Beauvais, blue terra-cotta in Burgundy, glazed terra-cotta for the high-necked, spherical, or oval jugs of Puisaye.

At the end of the nineteenth century, faience manufacturers such as Hamage, Sarreguemines, Clairefontaine, Dèvres, Salins, Saint-Amand, and Saint-Clément, which had enthusiastically embraced the new vogue for barbotine, began producing jugs depicting droll human or animal forms and themes. In northern France, Orchies came up with an original line of unexpected creatures like moray eels, swans, and donkeys. But perhaps the most interesting and the most carefully crafted pitchers of all came from the pottery of Onnaing, near Valenciennes. Onnaing's production was highly varied, with animals treated wittily, along with famous people of the period and professions—sailors, railroad workers, miners, and monks. These pitchers tended to be lined in red.

A distinct curiosity was the *pichet trompeur* or trick jug. This piece had a hollow handle, attached to a hollow rim extending all round the perforated neck of the jug, which made it possible to suck the liquid directly into the mouth—provided that a little hole under the handle was blocked with the thumb. Malicorne produced large numbers of these.

Champagne Buckets

Coolers made of precious metals, faience, and porcelain underwent a transformation in the nineteenth century to emerge as buckets for chilling champagne on ice. Most were made of cut crystal with a rim encircled by metal, which became silver plate after 1850. They were shaped like small conical or cylindrical casks, with or without a low stand; they had lugs, ring-handles, or knobs on the side for carrying. A similar type of bucket, though narrower and taller, was used for chilling Rhine wine. Other table utensils relating to champagne were the cork gripper and the cork with movable or static rings.

TIPS FOR COLLECTORS

Old bottles are all the more valuable because they are handmade. Their irregularities of shape and color make them highly sought after by collectors.

Marks of wear and tear are perfectly acceptable on a very old piece.

Eighteenth-century carafes are lighter than ones from the nineteenth century. Sometimes you can make out the trace of the glassblowers' pontil rod on the bottom of a carafe—a proof that it is genuinely old.

Nineteenth-century carafes are not particularly prized and so are plentiful and affordable. Check that the stopper is the original one made for the piece: there should be no play between the stopper and the neck of the carafe, and the decoration on the body of the carafe should be reproduced on the stopper.

Among the most common themes for pitchers are roosters, dogs, and owls.

Taking care of carafes and pitchers

To clean the inside, mix white vinegar and coarse salt, shake thoroughly, allow to soak for a while, and rinse.

For the exterior, use burning alcohol, window cleaner, or acetone. Never stopper a wet carafe.

If the stopper gets stuck in the neck, apply a few drops of oil.

5.

6.

7.

8.

ETYMOLOGY

In eighteenth-century France, the word **gobelet** could mean a mug as well as a glass, or a goblet. You could drink from a **gobelet à** lait, (milk mug), a **gobelet à café** (coffee mug), or a **gobelet à chocolat** (chocolate mug).

Cups and Water Goblets

In the old days, the water goblet was soberly married to the wine glass and was slightly bigger. Today it is freed of that bondage. Double-crystal goblets, tinted or delicately enameled glasses, and silver or porcelain mugs are all fine for an original table setting.

The Cup

From the remotest antiquity, the cup has been a cylindrical drinking cup, taller than it is wide, without a handle and often without a foot, with or without a cover, and mainly used for drinking water. It began small, with thick and smooth, or ribbed sides; later, in the Middle Ages, it became a luxury item of gold or silver, sometimes studded with precious stones. As such it featured strongly on the tables of the great, where it would be shared by several guests at a time. During the Renaissance, it lengthened and became a kind of tankard, a valuable, richly worked receptacle made variously of wood, pewter, porcelain, precious metal, rock crystal, or glass and was often personalized with an inscribed date or event. In the seventeenth century it sobered up, but in the eighteenth century, it was a standard feature of every aristocratic table: with or without a foot and stem, in porcelain, faience, or glass—preferably Bohemian cut glass. At the beginning of the nineteenth century, the cup was encrusted with stones and later with medallions, figurines, or cut panels obtained by the pressed glass technique. After 1830, the crystal water goblet, usually with a stem and matching the other components of a set, took the place of the cup.

Timbale or the Metal Cup

The French word *timbale* appeared at the end of the eighteenth century to distinguish a drinking cup made of metal from one made of glass, faience, or porcelain. But the object itself had already been in existence for many centuries. During the Renaissance it took the form of a truncated cone and was rather rustic looking. In the early seventeenth century it acquired a foot and stem, which made it look more elegant, though its body remained dead straight. By the eighteenth century, the sides of the cup were bell- or tulip-shaped, with lambrequin decorations characteristic of the period. Under Louis XV rocaille took over, with *piédouche* (the "foot") ever more finely worked. Under Louis XVI the cup became taller and straighter in outline, with designs drawn from nature. By the end of the eighteenth century and during the Empire period, the *timbale* had once again become cylindrical, with no stem or foot, but with a flat, smooth bottom. When it was small, ultrasimple, and with rounded angles, it was called *cul rond* ("round-bottomed").

In the nineteenth century, three types of *timbale* drinking cups were in use: *à piédouche* ("with a foot and stem"), *goblet droit* ("straight-sided"), and *cul rond*. With the invention of silver plate, they became

2.

3.

4.

1. Water glasses, 20th century.

2. Japanese-style glass, circa 1880.

3. Bohemian cut-glass with flat sides, 1860.

4. Bohemian double crystal cure glass, 1860.

1.

2.

1. *Timbales*, or metal drinking cups: conical, with bee frieze; plain doucine; doucine with twisted grooves and boss beading; conical with straight grooves; conical with ribbon fillets; with bent ribs; telescopic traveling cup; cactus; and flat-sided traveling cup.

2. Assorted water glasses.

3. Short glasses used as candle jars.

4. Late-19th-century, silver-plated cup; two 19th-century, sterling silver cups; and a 20th-century, sterling silver cup.

standard family heirlooms when people started giving them to children as christening gifts, presented in a case and engraved with the name of the recipient. They also came accompanied by a napkin ring, an eggcup with matching spoon, a dish, a teacup, dessert knife, fork, and spoon, and a coffee spoon. Their eclectic designs were inspired by the different styles of the past and could be very elaborate. In the 1920s, the *timbale* bowed to the more sober and elegant criteria of the time and reverted to its former identity as a discreet drinking cup.

TIPS FOR COLLECTORS

The choice of cups and water goblets is quite frankly infinite, as are their materials, shapes, colors, and origins.

Rather than buying a brand new **timbale**, it may be more interesting to seek out an attractive antique one. A dent or two can add a certain charm. The most sought-after **timbales** are old ones, with sophisticated designs, perhaps dating from the Empire and the Restoration. Appliqué decorations are particularly prized, and **timbales** from Strasbourg—which was famous for its silversmiths—are also at a premium today, as are antique pieces by the Parisian silversmiths Berti, Burron, Chéret, Delannoy, Tassin, and Thonelier. Joubert of Angers, Bataille and Béchard of Orleans, and Busnel, Le Mire, and Roussel of Rouen are other well-known names.

2.

3.

4.

Nineteenth-Century Crystal Stemware

Crystal stemware from the nineteenth century came in many forms, from cut crystal glasses reflecting the light from a thousand facets, to infinitely delicate engraved crystal, gilded crystal, and lined crystal of unearthly visual depth. We have yet to find a more exquisite means of making our table beautiful than to load it with these small, slender-stemmed masterpieces.

Orgues du Plaisir

Until the eighteenth century, glasses were not set on the dining table but kept in racks on the side. The diners called servants to bring them a glass of wine, immediately handing it back when it was drained. The one drinking cup was used by several different people, and in the more distant past it was no more than a simple cup made of metal or ceramic. In the reign of Louis XIV, glasses appeared whose sizes were specially adapted to the drink they were supposed to contain. They were known as *orgues du plaisir* ("organs of pleasure") and were extravagantly luxurious pieces, taking a proud place on a side table or dining table, but not always assigned to individual guests: they were shared by all. It was only from about 1880 onward that diners were each provided with three to six glasses of the same pattern and decoration, positioned in a diamond, rectangular, or square formation in front of their plate and attended by matching carafes.

The new trend inspired crystal makers to new heights of creativity, which had its effect not only on the shapes but also on the decoration of the glass, not to mention the use of white glass, tinted glass, and lined crystal. Before long you could obtain sets of water tumblers, beer glasses, glasses for different red wines, Madeira glasses, liqueur glasses, champagne glasses (in the shape of a coupe or a flute, these were used as early as the sixteenth century in Lorraine), and even "impossible" glasses (also known as *culs secs* or "dry bottoms"), which had nothing to stand on and so had to be drained in one gulp. All these glassware were blown individually and hand-decorated by glassmakers.

Blown Crystal

Glass and crystal both come from the fusion of a vitrifying element (silica or sand), a melting element (sodium carbonate, potassium, red oxide of lead) and a stabilizing element.

To shape a glass, the glassblower begins with a parison, or small bubble of molten glass. The exact quantity of melting crystal needed to make a particular stage of the glass is scooped on to the end of the slender blowpipe. The air is blown into the blowpipe, and the glass takes its form. Once the parison is created, the master glassblower places the stem on the wine glass, using a small quantity of crystal brought to him by another craftsman; after which he stretches it and gives it its final shape. Next, following the same sequence

5.

of actions, another glassblower brings the molten crystal needed to attach the foot of the glass. Once shaping of the glass is finished, it is detached from the pipe and refired, after which it is carefully examined—and thrown away if it presents the smallest imperfection. After this "hot" stage of manufacture comes the "cold" stage—the decoration stage.

Cut Glass

Cutting is one of the oldest techniques for decorating glass, and it allows the material to absorb the light and better refract it. Because of this process, it gives the impression of sparkling from hundreds of different angles.

The cutter uses a diamond grinder, a pumice, sandstone, or Carborundum stone to score the surface of the glass. Designs are reproduced fixed on a board, tracing all manner of motifs: flat, fluted, or diamond points (the Trianon pattern made by the Saint-Louis glassworks blends flat sides with diamond points), medallions, pearls, olives, fillets, bands, lozenges, festoons, and draperies. Once the cutting is completed, the glass is moved on to the polishing stage, which is carried out mechanically by a cork disk, or by immersion in a batch of acid, whereby its rough edges are removed and its surfaces smoothed.

Engraved Glass

Cold engraving, also known as sand engraving, is done with a thin jet of sand directed against the surface of the glass. With the use of a stencil, only the exposed areas are touched. Chemical engraving, which was perfected in 1860, is done with acid. Wheel engraving is done with a copper wheel cooled with water or with a grinder. Specialists engrave all kinds of motifs on glass, such as flowers, friezes, nature and mythological scenes, geometric designs, checkers, monograms, and coats of arms.

Tinted Glass

Coloration can be obtained in two ways. The first is by tinting in mass, by adding metal oxides at the time of firing. This coloration begins from the presence of metallic ions in the crystal during melting (cobalt oxide gives blue, chrome oxide gives green, tin oxide gives white, nickel oxide and potassium give purple, copper oxide gives turquoise, and copper oxide plus gold chloride gives ruby).

Coloration can also be obtained by adding mineral components that do not dissolve in the mix during the melting process, but which, as the mix cools, form fine particles within it. These minerals cause the light to diffract and produce rich tinting effects: ruby for gold, red for copper, yellow for silver, and pink for selenium. Glasses tinted this way became very fashionable after 1830. Between 1837 and 1845, Saint-Louis revived the filigree technique and produced articles in previously untried materials such as alabaster or aventurine. The Saint-Louis glassworks also perfected opaline crystal, which all the great glassmakers were to reproduce in the later nineteenth century.

Double-Crystal Glass

Double-, triple-, and even multi-layered crystal, which are specialties of the glassmakers of Bohemia, are made by superimposing hot layers of crystal onto others, according to a predetermined design. In double-crystal glass, one layer is colored, the other is not. The technique is the same as the one used to make the Rhine wine glasses, which the Germans call *roemer*. This type of glass, which has existed since the fourteenth century, started out as a bulky goblet decorated with cabochons. In the nineteenth century, it acquired an ample hollow stem, and at the beginning of the twentieth century, it became significantly taller. Blue, red, and pistachio green are the most common colors for double crystal, which is often cut, filigreed, or wheel engraved—though it also exists in rarer tones like amber or copper-gold. The wine glasses of Alsace, which are long-stemmed with small bowls, are nearly always made of double crystal.

Enameled Glass

A strong presence in Islamic art from the twelfth to the fourteenth century, in the Ottoman Empire and Damascus and then

2.

3.

4.

1.　2.　3.　4.　5.

1. Double crystal enameled glass. Bohemia.

2. Bohemian gold and enameled molded glass, 19th century.

3. Gold and enameled glass. Bohemia, 1850.

4. Colored crystal stemware, Louis-Philippe period.

5. Ruby glass. Bohemia, 1860.

6. Assortment of cut-crystal champagne glasses.

7. Cut-crystal, diamond-point liqueur set, engraved and gilded, 19th century.

Following pages :

1. Colored cut-crystal glasses for white wine.

2. Guilloched crystal stemware. Manufacture de Bayel, 19th century.

3. Richly engraved German glass with vegetable motifs and coat of arms, 17th century.

4. Engraved, lightly tinted glass with a chateau design, 19th century.

5. Wine and orange soda glasses, cut crystal, early 20th century.

in Renaissance Venice, painted enamel is applied by hand to the surface of the glass, which is then fired at a temperature of about 850°F. Sometimes the piece is not refired, which renders the enamel much more fragile.

Gilded Glass

Gold decoration applied to crystal glasses first made its appearance around 1880. It tended to be restricted to really fine sets because it involved hand-brushing a precious layer of gold on to the glass, and then refiring it at a temperature of about 900°F. When the glass comes out of the kiln, its gilded areas appear matte textured, and their luster must be revived by rubbing with red iron ore.

TIPS FOR COLLECTORS

The crystal glasses manufactured today cost considerably more than the same patterns bought secondhand.

Red wine and water glasses are more sought after than white wine, port, or liqueur glasses, which are used less often. Very deep cutting indicates that the glass dates from the end of the nineteenth century or the early twentieth century. The most sought-after crystal glasses are from the period of Louis-Philippe.

If the enamel of a glass is in any way impaired, the glass loses much of its value.

Taking care of glassware

Crystal glasses can be washed in the dishwasher if certain precautions are taken: Do not wash them with silver or crockery.

Use a light cycle for glasses and use a very gentle detergent. .

When ordinary glasses are mixed with other tableware, there is a risk of dulling, due to the combination of certain detergents with water of poor quality.

Repairing broken glassware

Rub the areas to be joined with sandpaper to make the surfaces as smooth as possible. Heat the glass in very hot water for one minute. Wipe quickly, apply a thin layer of Superglue or Krazy Glue on one of the two broken edges to be glued, and apply the other edge.

Repairing a broken stem

It is best to leave this task to a professional. However, if you must do it yourself, first clean and dry the two pieces. Lay the top of the glass upside down on a clean cloth. Adjust the foot on top of it. Hold the two parts together with a thick roll of clay or plasticine to support the foot. Apply a drop of water-resistant synthetic glue to the cup section, taking care not to let the glue run: if it does, remove the excess with a matchstick. Allow to dry for twenty-four hours.

Repairing a small chip

Polish the chipped edge with medium-grain sandpaper rolled around the shaft of a pencil. If the chip is too big, leave the work to a professional.

Separating a glass stuck inside another

Plunge the lower glass into hot water, then immediately fill the upper one with cold; then pull gently to separate the two.

2.

3.

1.

Art Deco Glassware

With their straight lines, simple forms, and discreet ornamentations, art deco glasses are astonishingly modern, a perfect match for contemporary tableware and silverware.

The Taste for Simplicity

During the International Decorative Arts Exhibition in Paris in 1925, a number of artists working with glass demonstrated their collective preference for form over ornament, the innate beauty of materials over their decoration, and transparency over color.

A case in point was Jean Luce, who, after serving his apprenticeship with the firm acquired by his father in 1888, founded a company of his own in 1901. Luce designed sets of china for several different factories, Sèvres among them, and it was he who first had the idea of matching glassware with ceramics, silverware, and even table linen. He created several sets of porcelain and crystal for the liner *Normandie* and collaborated with the Saint-Louis glassworks, for which he invented his *Hossegor* and *Eva* patterns, which are quintessential art deco. Saint-Louis committed itself to this modernist movement by commissioning other artists such as Jean Sala, from a famous dynasty of Italian glassmakers, Maurice Dufrene, Marcel Goupy, and Max Ingrand.

Baccarat responded with the great designer Georges Chevalier, who came up with his very own ultralight muslin glasses. These were conical or slightly flared and tuliplike, with a parison of extraordinary purity. Chevalier also designed sets of stable, stemless glasses with broad, thick bases, especially for wealthy yacht owners. His *Jets d'eau* service was a model of sobriety and harmony, with parisons etched with acid representing stylized streams of water, and stems and feet decorated with frosted and molded flower patterns.

The Reign of Lalique

Without a doubt, the dominant figure of the era was Rene Lalique. Lalique's first research into glass and crystal dated from 1890, when he was still a jeweler by trade. In 1902, he made some molded glass panels for his townhouse at Cours-la-Reine, and in 1906, Francois Coty commissioned him to design perfume bottles, which were made by Legras at Saint-Denis. After this project, Lalique set up his own workshop and in 1911 gave up jewelry altogether to concentrate on glass, reacting against overuse of color and working skillfully around the contrast between transparent and burnished glass. He was the inventor of a particularly strong "half-crystal," which had both the luster and the transparency of traditional crystal. His glasses were simple in construction, with refined outlines; he successfully applied his manufacturing methods to vases, decorative panels, and table services, and his firm supplied all the glass for the *Normandie*'s most luxurious staterooms.

Daum, another famous name, began producing crystal in 1934 with an order for one hundred thousand pieces—again for the *Normandie*. The Daum glassworks was a leading light of art nouveau decoration and eventually specialized more in decorative crystal than in drinking glasses. Choisy-le-Reine and Val Saint-Lambert, whose most gifted designers were Simonet and Marcel Goupy respectively, also produced very beautiful art deco glasses, as did Pantin, Clichy, and Sèvres.

3.

1. Detail of the foot of an orange soda glass. Cristal Lalique, 1920–1930. (Lalique pieces are always signed).

2. Detail of the foot of a glass from Lalique's *Nippon* service. Cristal Lalique, 20th century.

3. Unsigned art deco glasses are often found in secondhand shops, selling at reasonable prices. This model is by Saint-Louis.

TIPS FOR COLLECTORS

Genuine Lalique pieces are all signed. Glass by Jean Luce appears on the market only on very rare occasions. Some of the original art deco designs are still produced today by Saint-Louis and Baccarat.

Bistrot Glasses

Bistrot glasses are modest in aspect, in stark contrast to spectacular table crystal; but this modesty is very much a virtue, given that they are invariably well designed and perfectly adapted to the drinks they are meant to contain. Used as part of a table setting, they have a way of making the occasion informal; you can almost feel the friendly bistro atmosphere surrounding them.

Absinthe Glasses

The "Green Fairy" absinthe, a potent blend of the diluted essences of Artemisia, aniseed, and fennel mixed with alcohol, was originally sold in French pharmacies before it became publicly available in bars, cafés, and wine shops. The first absinthe was created in the Doubs department of France by Pernod Fils—and caused much havoc and misery before it was banned on March 6, 1915, for the very good reason that it drove people mad. The traditional absinthe glass had a stem and a conical shape with thick sides. It came with a small, slotted spoon; this was laid across the rim with a lump of sugar in it, over which water was poured drop by drop until the precise moment when absinthe beneath turned cloudy.

Martini Glasses

The martini glass was also conical, with thick sides.

The Shot Glass

Stemmed shot glasses were intentionally small, only meant to contain a very small quantity of alcohol. You could always order a second.

Tankards and Beer Glasses

The tankard, which was traditionally made in eastern and northern France, had a cover to keep the beer at the right tepid temperature. In the Middle Ages, it was heavily and ornately decorated; later in the sixteenth century, it spread all over Europe, adopting a cylindrical shape with a pewter cover. In more recent times, porcelain tankards were produced by factories, such as Hannong of Strasbourg, in eastern France. From the nineteenth century onward, people began serving beer in tall, thick glasses, and as the years went by, the glasses were adapted to specific types of beer. Thus a frothy brew came in a tulip-shaped glass, Belgian beer arrived in a round goblet on a stem, and ordinary cylindrical glasses were used for ordinary pale lagers. Later, the breweries began distributing glasses advertising their own brands and logos, which were immediately adopted by the bars.

Lemonade Glasses

Originally from southern France, lemonade glasses were thick, shaped like a truncated cone, and etched with broad diamonds.

The Voleur Glass

This curiosity was also known as *verre du patron* ("host's glass"), or *verre faux-cul* ("cheating glass") because it allowed the bar owners to drink with their customers while consuming less alcohol. It had a solid glass bottom and thick sides, which meant that it could contain only the minimum amount of alcohol.

2.

1. Molded cider and lemonade glasses, assorted motifs.

2. Three Bohemian crystal beer mugs with pewter additions, 19th century.

1.

The Mazagran, Coffee Glasses, and Burned-Brandy Glasses

The Mazagran glass was named after a town in Algeria, where a French garrison of 123 chasseurs commanded by the gallant Capitaine Lièvre managed to repel an army of fourteen thosand men under Sheik Abd el-Kader. The French troopers were fortified during their ordeal by scalding hot coffee laced with sugar and eau-de-vie. To commemorate their feat of arms, a factory in Bourges created and marketed a large, thick-sided porcelain cup called a "Mazagran."

Coffee is still occasionally served in French cafés in a glass with thick sides to keep it hot. The shape is the same as that of a Mazagran.

The *brulot* (burned brandy) glass, or *tasse de bistrot* ("bistro cup"), is made of thick porcelain and has the same heat-retaining function, provided it is heated well before the liquid is poured in. Other hot drinks are also consumed from this kind of cup.

Verre de curiste or the "Spa Glass"

In the last quarter of the nineteenth century, it became ultrafashionable to drink the waters annually at French spa towns such as Aix-les-Bains. At the start of a treatment, the patients would be presented with a glass—sometimes calibrated—and usually engraved with the name of the spa. They then kept it for the duration of the entire treatment, carrying it in a sling over their shoulders or at their belts, in a small wickerwork pouch.

TIPS FOR COLLECTORS

Old **bistrot** glasses, so conducive to geniality and friendliness, are becoming hard to find—and their prices are going up as well. Don't hesitate to snap up individual pieces if they appeal to you. They can only increase in value.

2.

3.

4.

5.

1.

2.

3.

4.

Pressed Glass

Their colors are enchanting to many; their heaviness can be inconvenient to some; and their price is reasonable all around the world. Pressed glass, which resembles cut glass, were mechanically produced in large numbers. It's time to rediscover their beauty.

Instead of Cutting

For centuries cutting was the most favored technique for decorating glasses. Cut glass was the height of fashion at the beginning and end of the nineteenth century, when makers like Baccarat were producing richly ornamented pieces of heavy crystal. The invention of a process for pressing glass with a machine supplied a fair imitation of cut glass that was considerably cheaper. It involved pouring molten glass into a mold bearing the ornamental details in relief, and pressing it with a counter-mold harnessed to a piston. The glass that emerged would be smooth on the inside and sculpted on the outside.

This technique was perfected in the United States in 1820 by the New England Glass Company. It was then immediately copied by its bitter rival, the Boston and Sandwich Glass Company in Cape Cod, Massachusetts, which employed a number of artisans from Europe. The latter produced pressed glass in such quantity that before long "sandwich glass" became the common name for American pressed glass in general. An impressive variety of objects emerged from the molds: bowls, dishes, vases, compotes, candlesticks,

fruit bowls, and cups and glasses of all sizes. They were engraved, like their hand-cut models, with sides that were flat or patterned with stars, diamonds, bevels, and squares. They also came in splendid colors such as cobalt blue, green, amber, and turquoise.

Around 1830, the pressed glass technique spread to Europe, notably by major glass producers such as Baccarat and Saint-Louis.

TIPS FOR COLLECTORS

Pieces made by glass pressing, such as water tumblers and goblets and colored candlesticks, are very decorative on a table, though their weight and, occasionally, their excessive ornamentations may not suit everyone's taste. In any event, pressed glass can be purchased at reasonable prices today, though its value is steadily on the rise.

The shapes of mechanically pressed glass are more uniform than those of hand-cut glass.

Pressed glass always carries the vertical impression of the joints of its mold.

5.

6.

1. Italian pressed glass.

2. Glass candy dish, early 20th century.

3 and 5. Candlesticks and pressed dishes, 19th century.

4. Different designs for pressed glasses.

6. Night-light, 19th century.

TABLE ACCESSORIES

This is a broad field offering plenty of possibilities for fun, self-expression, and originality. All the more so since nowadays, people no longer have any reservations about mixing styles, materials, and periods to create a desirable table and are ready to find and embrace inspirations wherever they may be.

Basically anything goes, so you can pick and choose from the vast quantities of items available. Certain traditions still remain, and that is not a bad thing—for example, we still like to dine by candlelight. You might opt for a pair of thoroughly eighteenth-century candelabras, or nonmatching sconces, or candle jars set at intervals around the table. And it is equally fashionable to arrange individual bouquets of flowers in metal cups by every place setting or place a big cut-glass bowl on a stem, piled high with fruit as a centerpiece.

Then there is the indispensable trio of salt cellar, pepper mill, and mustard pot—which have inspired so many artisans all through the ages. They come in every shape and size, from staid and conventional to completely outlandish, as do place mats and hot plates, and all their kin. There are also cohorts of smaller accessories—menu holders, place cards, knife rests, and so on; the possibilities are endless.

Candlesticks and Candelabras

Dinner by candlelight is always a delight, with its power to make silver and crystal glitter, faces look glamorous, and eyes shine. Candle jars may be very fashionable today, but there is still a lot to be said for the grand candelabras and candlesticks of the past—made of fine materials and beautifully crafted.

Candlestick or Girandole?

The French word *chandelier* does not necessarily mean a cluster of lights or candles suspended from the ceiling, as it does in English. Instead it describes anything in which a candle can be placed. The small portable candleholder is its simplest form. The French *flambeau* is more precise: it is a candlestick with a single holder. In the seventeenth century, *flambeau* became the customary word for a vertical stem with a circular or polygonal foot, a candle socket on top, and no handle. The candelabra, by contrast, is a candleholder with several branches, while the girandole is a ornamental candelabra whose stem is composed of human figures. It can also describe a candelabra with cut-glass pendants. As for the French *bougeoir* (a flat candlestick), it appeared around 1824 with the invention of the wax candle.

Eighteenth-Century Shapes and Outlines

When the tallow candle was invented in the Middle Ages, it brought with it the *flambeau* candlestick. Prior to that time, a *flambeau* in French meant a blazing oil torch on a stick, used to light the way along dark streets at night. By the seventeenth century, the *flambeau* candlestick had already assumed the form we recognize today: a fluted, square-cut, or balustered stem, set on a broad base, square or with the corners cut off.

At the end of the century, the French introduced a technique for molding candlesticks in sterling silver, with base and stems separately made, then soldered or—more rarely—screwed together. At this time, ornamentation entered the equation. In the eighteenth century, the faience and porcelain makers of Rouen, Moustiers, Saint-Cloud, and Sèvres began making candlesticks whose shapes were based on those of gold and silverware, with decorations of a piece with their styles. As the century wore on, these shapes evolved. Next came two-branched candelabras, then appeared candlesticks with multiple branches with sophisticated designs devised by famous silver and gold workers for the tables of the great. Many of these formed diminutive elements of a gigantic table centerpiece. Imagination and flawless craftsmanship were at a premium during the reign of Louis XV, with the coming of a flamboyant rocaille style based on intertwined candelabra branches and asymmetrical ornamentation

Shapes and decorations only settled down at the end of the century, with the return to neoclassicism under Louis XVI. While the candelabras flooded tables with glittering light, pairs of candlesticks were placed on fireplaces on either side of clocks. They were made of sterling silver, bronze, silver, or gold plate and consisted of three sections—base, stem, and candle socket—screwed together to form a single entity.

2.

1.

2.

3.

4.

1, 3, and 4. Designs for
Louis XV-style candelabras

2. Louis XVI-style candelabra.

5. Design for a four-armed
candelabra by Cardeilhac for
Christofle, 1925–1930.

6. Assorted molded glass and
crystal candlesticks, late 19th and
early 20th century.

7. Assorted candlesticks, 19th to
20th century.

8. Assortment of French and
English sterling silver candlesticks,
18th century.

The Nineteenth Century: the Age of Decorum

During the First Empire, leading craftsmen, such as Odiot, were inspired by antiquity to produce pieces with fluted or balustered stems, and silver gave way to gilded bronze and vermeil. However, with the invention of silver electroplating, the decorum-obsessed Second Empire developed a predilection for large decorative candelabras based on models from the reigns of Louis XIV and Louis XV, such as those made by Christofle and Boin-Taburet. Meanwhile glassmakers such as Saint-Louis and Baccarat were producing immense chandeliers, decked with thousands of glass pendants, for the townhouses of the rich and the palaces of princes.

Curious Oddities

The *amusoir* or "flycatcher" is a glass candelabra incorporating a water-filled container for drowning flies attracted by the light. The candlesnuffer is a metal rod with a small hollow cap at its end for dousing candles. Scissors snuffers were used to snip blackened wicks, which fell neatly into a little metal box attached to one blade.

TIPS FOR COLLECTORS

Candlesticks and candelabras predating the Revolution—meaning they escaped the wholesale melting down of silver to pay for France's wars—are few and far between these days. They are usually sold in pairs today, which adds to their value.

When a silver candelabra is composed of several sections, check that each section bears the same hallmark. Also verify that the sockets are the original ones and that all the branches are intact—these can be very awkward to repair.

Nineteenth-century, silver-plated copies of older candlesticks and candelabras are plentiful on the market, and many go for bargain prices.

Oil lamps made of blown glass, which were produced in Provence during the 1830s, make very attractive candleholders.

5.

Centerpieces

Table centerpieces have never gone out of style. In the eighteenth century, the trend was for the precious *cadenas* (shackled casket); in the nineteenth century, the towering *surtout* predominated. Today the choice of what to place in the middle of a dinner table is a matter of individual taste and imagination.

Nefs and Cadenas

The ancestors of centerpiece were the *nef* and the *cadenas*. From the Middle Ages through to the late sixteenth century, the most spectacular item on the royal table was the *cadenas*, a gold or silver casket with a shackle to discourage assassination by poison. Along with a set of antidotes to various toxins, it contained the king's napkin, his flatware, and assorted small vessels containing spices, salt, and sugar, all of which were rare and precious commodities. These small vessels were couched in a boat-shaped receptacle, the *nef*. The most celebrated of these was the one designed by Le Brun and made by Jean Gravet for Louis XIV.

From Surtout to Présentoir

The French word *surtout* first surfaced in 1692, in a description of the festivities surrounding the wedding of the Duc de Chartres. It designated a single piece of silver or gold work that brought together the salt cellar, spice box, oil pitcher, and vinegar jug with various vases, candleholders, sconces, and candelabras. Throughout the eighteenth century, this spectacular object accompanied the tableware delivered to the courts of Europe and the houses of wealthy aristocrats by the greatest living craftsmen in silver and gold (Louis XIV's *surtout* was made by Delaunay).

In the nineteenth century, the surtout lost its utilitarian function and became purely decorative, while remaining a fixture throughout the meal. Sometimes it covered the whole length of the table and represented a nature scene from mythology or the hunting chase; it might also be a skillfully engineered construction made from a large number of sculpted components, placed on a platter with a mirror bottom representing a lake. It could be made of gold, silver, crystal, biscuit, or porcelain.

The vogue for these elaborate pieces died away at the Restoration of the French monarchy. They were replaced by dessert services, comprised of series of cut-glass fruit stands on stems of different heights made of beautifully worked metal. These stems were sculpted in the forms of children, or animals and were topped by a high crystal cone entirely filled with fruits or cakes. Dessert services were accompanied by stands with several tiers and baskets and candelabras mass-produced by firms such as Christofle. They offered plenty of options for flights of fancy: "white glass bowls filled with water, with goldfish and baby turtles swimming about, are quite the thing these days," noted a late-nineteenth-century lifestyle manual.

The twentieth century sternly jettisoned all such extravagance, preferring the unostentatious display of a vase of flowers and plain but refined candlesticks.

TIPS FOR COLLECTORS

Big, impressive, complete **surtouts** are no longer interesting to anyone but specialist collectors. Even so, it is not unusual to come across odds and ends of old ones, in the form of crystal, biscuitware statuettes, porcelain figurines, woven silver baskets, and the like.

2.

3.

4.

1. Fine porcelain Medici mini-vases, for table decoration.

2. Centerpiece, with cornet and four cut-glass dishes.

3. Tall fruit stand with children and vine decoration.

4. Cut-crystal fruit stand on a silver-plated base.

1.

2.

3.

4.

Individual Accessories

Nothing is ruled out when it comes to an original table setting, especially the objects that have preserved real charm and personality though they may have gone out of fashion long ago.

Menu Holders and Menus

In the nineteenth century, when people gave dinner parties, it was customary to place a card with the evening's menu before each guest. The card was held vertically upright in a little stand with a clip on top, or was fitted into a metal frame. These small accessories were mass-produced in silver, tin, glass, brass, or china, and sometimes came with a matching holder for the card bearing the name of the guest.

The menu itself was created with the utmost care and included line drawings of landscapes, flowers, and figures on Japanese vellum, parchment, or a broad ribbon of colored satin placed in a glass.

The Knife Rest

Knife rests made their appearance in the second half of the nineteenth century. They were a bourgeois invention, enabling diners to keep the same knife for several successive courses and eliminating the need to change the tablecloth for each new meal. They came in many forms, from the diminutive rectangle in earthenware, porcelain, and cut crystal, to the match-stick-sized silver rod with bobbles, rings, or claws at either end. The knife rest also lent itself to fanciful portrayals of fish, dogs, and birds; the animals of La Fontaine's fables were all pressed into dinnerware, as were those of Benjamin Rabier.

The Napkin Ring

The napkin ring made it possible for people to identify their own napkin for the next meal and the next. It tended to be used within families, rather than for dinner or lunch parties when outsiders were invited. Like the knife rest, the napkin ring first appeared in the nineteenth century and was often given to babies at their birth

along with a silver drinking cup and an eggcup. Like the latter, it might be in sterling silver, silver plate, nickel-plated copper, aluminum, ivory, horn, ceramic, wood, or even flexible celluloid. Since the napkin ring was a personal object, it was often engraved with a Christian name or initials.

The Finger Bowl

The finger bowls first came into general use around 1760, along with the habit of eating shellfish and crustaceans. In general it was an opaque crystal bowl occupying a small tray of its own. In the nineteenth century, it was frequently accompanied by a three-piece mouth-rinsing set, which included a small crystal bowl, a saucer, and a goblet that could be filled with a mixture of water and mint or lemon-flavored alcohol. Guests would take a mouthful of this brew from the goblet, rinse it round their teeth, and spit it discreetly into the bowl. "In many houses, a sterilized quill toothpick is laid on the cloth to the right of each guest, wrapped in tissue paper. I formally admonish ladies not to make use of these, because personally I find the habit of picking the teeth publicly after a meal most unattractive. For the same reason, the finger bowl no longer appears with the little cup people once used to rinse their mouths," notes an early-twentieth-century-lifestyle manual. But the finger bowls themselves are still essential objects for our tables.

TIPS FOR COLLECTORS

Napkin rings are used less and less nowadays, with paper napkins having largely taken the place of cloth ones. On the other hand, these attractive, inexpensive items seem to be making a comeback for intimate meals among friends.

5.

---

1. Silver-plated metal knife rests, 1940–1950.

2. Souvenir napkin rings, 1920s.

3. Spade-shaped knife rests, 1950s.

4. Porcelain knife rest, 1930s.

5. Assorted knife rests offered in the 1913 Christofle catalogue. Prices varied between 16.5 and 40 francs per dozen at that time.

2.

Salt Cellars, Mustard Pots, and Cruets

The salt, side by side with the pepper; the mustard in its little pot; the oil and vinegar in their sophisticated cruet—they have all been faithfully present at our meals for generations now. No receptacle is too good for them.

3.

Salt Cellars

In the Middle Ages, salt made it possible to preserve meat and vegetables. It was a rare and expensive commodity in France, subject to a tax of its own. It also had a symbolic religious value, representing a mystical alliance between God and his people. For this reason, it was out of the question for anyone in a position of importance to keep his salt in a commonplace container. Salt cellars were prestige items, made of gold, encrusted with precious stones, and decorated with symbols.

In the sixteenth century, the salt cellars gradually lost its religious mystique and began to be decorated in a style more in keeping with salt's natural origin—sea gods, sea symbols, and fish. This trend reached its crowning moment with the vogue for rocaille, which had salt nestling in containers resembling seashells and decorated with motifs of marine life. The most celebrated example was produced by Thomas Germain, which was covered in sculpted crabs, turtles, and scallops. Marie-Antoinette launched a trend for tiny blue crystal salt bowls set in perforated silver base, with matching mustard pots. The nineteenth century saw the arrival of the *Cérébos* salt cellar or salt shaker, made of ribbed or smooth crystal with a screw-on, perforated metal top.

4.

This, of course, is the basic design that remains in use today.

Pepper Pots and Pepper Mills

In the eighteenth century, salt and pepper began to be presented together in a twin "double cellar" made of silver or glass with a silver base. The table pepper mill, again made of silver or glass, did not emerge until the nineteenth century. Other spices that were so prized in the seventeenth century gradually fell out of favor, and by the end of the eighteenth century, only cloves, nutmeg, and cinnamon remained on the table, in a spice box that had several compartments.

Mustard Pots

Mustard has been used as a condiment in Europe since the thirteenth century. In eighteenth-century France, it was sold on the streets by children who transported it in casks, using wheelbarrows. For this reason, the first table mustard pots, which appeared around 1752, were shaped like tiny barrels. Madame de Pompadour had a pair of silver mustard pots made for her by the silversmith Antoine-Sébastien Durand, in the figure of cupid wheeling a barrel of mustard along in a delicately engraved barrow; beside the cupid is a greyhound standing on its hind legs.

5.

1. Crystal and silver-plate oil cruet.

2. Assorted silver-plated pepper mills.

3. Porcelain salt cellar and pepper pot, 1930s.

4. Sterling silver shakers by Keller, 19th ceutury.

5. Salt and pepper pots shaped like scallops, a seaside souvenir.

1. Assorted oil cruets, silver-plated metal frameworks and cut-glass bottles.

2. Salt and spice holders, silver-plated frames, cut-glass pots and bowls.

3. Mustard pot, cut-glass with a notched lid for the mustard spoon, late 19th century.

4. Design for a cylindrical pepper mill on three feet, 1889.

5. Design for a pear-shaped mustard pot with hinged lid, 1898.

6. Cut-glass oil and vinegar cruet, late 18th century.

In the nineteenth century, the mustard pot, as in the time of Marie-Antoinette, came in the form of a tiny tub of clear or dark blue crystal set in a heavily worked silver structure. It had a hinged lid and a side handle for opening the lid. Some of these lids had notches in them to accommodate a little mustard spoon.

From the late nineteenth century onward, salt cellars, pepper mills, and mustard pots—though they still matched and were brought together—lost their conventional character. Imagination ran wild as potters and porcelain manufacturers produced a large number of cheap, vividly colored, and often humorous variations on the themes of fruit, vegetables, crustaceans, animals, children, and different professions.

Oil and Vinegar Cruets

Gabrielle d'Estrées, the favorite of Henri IV, was unusually fond of vinegar and was the first to bring it to the dinner table. The earliest version of the combination oil and vinegar cruet was called a *guédoufle* and consisted of two transparent glass or crystal bottles, with entwined necks, set in an oval dish or on a broad, stable base. In the seventeenth century, oil and vinegar began to be presented in oval or octagonal boxes, whose tops contained four holes, two for the bottles and two for their stoppers. During the rocaille period, they gained oval platters with perforated mounts and cork holders and ornamentations of olive trees and vines to show their function. In the reign of Louis XVI, the platter became a tray and the bottles were blue crystal.

In the eighteenth century, cruet stands were of metal with a central stem topped by a handle and four rings—two large ones to hold the bottles, and two smaller ones for the stoppers. The same principle applied to the *ménagère* cruet stands of the early nineteenth century, some of which contained not only oil and vinegar but also salt, pepper, powdered sugar, and even mustard and pickles.

TIPS FOR COLLECTORS

The value of antique salt cellars, mustard pots, and oil cruets has remained more or less stable, though fine oil and vinegar cruets have become expensive.

With patience, it may be possible not only to find a cruet stand on its own, but also the cruets to fit it. Likewise, the stoppers, which is usually missing, can eventually be found one way or another.

4.

6.

2.

3.

4.

Ice Buckets, Glass Holders, and Hot Plates

These table accessories—jewels of the old domestic economy whose original purpose was always to make things easier for the household—have come back with a vengeance in recent years to the delight of anyone interested in the art of the table.

Ice Buckets, Glass Holders, and Coolers

In the eighteenth century, bottles and glasses never appeared on the table at all. Instead they were left on the side table, plunged into glass holders or coolers, ready to be carried to the guests when required. The buckets were made of silver, faience, or porcelain; they were round or oval, with crenellated rims to hold the bottles and glasses securely in place.

By the early nineteenth century, individual glasses and carafes moved to the table and the old coolers ceased to have any real purpose. Still, individual glass holders were used, according to the type of wine being served, either to cool a glass in ice or to warm it in tepid water. Ceramic manufacturers and leading goldsmiths and silversmiths, such as Charles-Nicolas Odiot and Boulenger, continued to make coolers and glass holders. Their elegance is timeless, which is why they are still in use even today as planters or centerpieces filled with fresh fruit or flowers.

Hot Plates

The hot plate was another nineteenth-century invention, which began as a decorative ceramic plaque, square or round in shape, with or without feet, and snugly fitted into a wooden casing. Some faience manufacturers produced fanciful versions of this useful object, with, for example, music boxes capable of playing one or two tunes or sliding casters for feet. Later, table hot plates came in wood, porcelain, pressed glass, or aluminum; certain models, made of nickel-plated copper, could be folded or opened out and had matching chafing dishes.

Coasters and Decanter Stands

These objects naturally came into being as soon as bottles and glasses made the leap from coolers and glass holders on the side table to the table proper. After all, it was important to protect the tablecloth from wine stains. Later, toward the end of the nineteenth century, these objects began to diversify.

1. Faience cistern used as a glass holder. Pont-aux-Choux or Rouen, 18th century.

2. Lacquered tin glass holder with Chinese decorations, circa 1765.

3. Hard-paste porcelain cooler. Manufacture Nast, 1783–1835.

4. Silver glass bucket by Auguste Robert-Joseph, 1778–1779.

1. Designs for silver-plated bells.

2. Silver hot plates and warmers.

3. Silver chafing dish, 19th century.

1.

2.

The simplest ones were aluminum or copper, and the most refined were silver plate or pressed and cut crystal with silver or wood bands. Generally, a small cross-piece of wood was set into the crystal to prevent the bottle from damaging it.

Chafing Dishes

The French were accustomed to laying their various cooked dishes on the table prior to the arrival of the guests. Even though many of them had fitted covers to keep them hot, chafing dishes were still a necessity. The eighteenth-century chafing dish sat on a metal stand over hot coals. In the nineteenth century, the stand was made of silver plate, and the heating was done by a candle or a small tub of burning alcohol with a wick in it. Some of the structures were no more than simple metal frames; others had four feet and were decorated in the same patterns as the hot plates, whose function they some-times shared. Especially interesting were silver vegetable dishes with built-in metal heating components. In the early twenti-eth century, goldsmiths and silversmiths began producing simple, candle-warmed metal chafing dishes.

Handbells and Gongs

To summon the servants between courses, the hostess would ring a small handbell made of silver, nickel-plated copper, deco-rated porcelain, or even cut crystal. The hostess would also slap a little gong with the flat of her hand or twist a button on it to and fro. An interesting variation was the table gong, a metal stand with a round piece of copper hanging on it, which was struck with a stick of boxwood.

2.

For Bread

Bread has been a staple of every European table since the Middle Ages and it occupies a vital if humble role as an accompaniment to many dishes. The bread basket is now a fixture everywhere, but other objects for bread have largely disappeared from the table.

Silent Butler

At the end of the nineteenth century, it was the general practice to clear away the bread crumbs on the table before serving the dessert (the French do not lay individual plates for bread like the English). The crumb clearing was done either with a crumb tray—a kind of straight-edged miniature shovel with a handle—or with a semicircular silent butler with a thumb catch. Both were used together with a long-handled soft brush.

In the reign of Napoleon III, many of these utensils were made of lacquered papier-mâché, but there are plenty of other variations in metal that have the standard range of decorations—seashells, palm leaves, ribbons, and garlands—as well as minor masterpieces of marquetry. The silent butler and brush were often made with matching bread baskets. In the 1920s, they were replaced by a single tool, a circular brush that was built into a silver-plated case.

The Bread Basket

The bread basket first appeared on the tables in France at the end of the eighteenth century. The early ones were oval or rectangular, occasionally square. When made of faience or porcelain, they tended to have an openwork design; when made of sterling silver, they were often decorated with appliqué motifs. Whatever the mate-

rial, the bread baskets were elegant, beautifully crafted objects that could just as easily be used for serving fruits and cakes instead of slices of bread. In the second half of the nineteenth century, the bread basket was frequently accompanied by the silent butler and its brush, all three being made of novel materials, such as silver plate, wood marquetry, or papier-mâché.

When imported Asian rattan and wickerwork were all the rage at the turn of the twentieth century, finely woven bread baskets of different colors began to appear. These were made not only of rattan, but plated silver that imitated the characteristics of woven rattan and wickerwork.

The Butter Board

This was a decorated piece of faience, with a hole at one end from which it could be hung on the wall. It was used for spreading butter or cheese on slices of bread.

3.

TIPS FOR COLLECTORS

Nowadays, silent butlers are rarely used outside restaurants, but they have plenty of appeal for enthusiasts, especially the Napoleon III lacquered variety, which can be collected as ornamental objects. Sold without its brush, or if the brush is in poor condition, the silent butler loses its market value but not its decorative quality.

1. Bread baskets made in older designs, 19th and 20th century.

2. Shell-shaped, spade-shaped, and Louis XV-style silent butlers.

3. Crumb scrapers: shell-shaped, swivel-sided, Louis XV, Empire, and Louis XV.

TEA, COFFEE, AND CHOCOLATE

Toward the end of the seventeenth century, three novelties revolutionized people's dining habits. All of Europe embraced these beverages from distant lands, and they soon became an inspiration to silversmiths, goldsmiths, and ceramists.

Tea from India and China was introduced to Europe by sailors working with the Dutch East India Company. The French discovered it around 1636. Louis XIV quickly became a fervent consumer, after receiving a solid gold teacup as a gift from the king of Siam. The tea drinking spread quickly among Europe's middle class beginning around 1840.

Coffee, originating in Abyssinia, arrived in Europe in the 1630s and began to be imported on a large scale to France via the port of Marseille in 1850. It quickly overtook tea as the preferred drink of the aristocracy, before becoming a staple of the cafés named in its honor.

Hernan Cortes was officially the first European to discover chocolatl in 1589, during his conquest of Mexico. This "food of the gods" arrived in France around 1670, following the marriage of the Infanta Anne of Austria to Louis XIII. Between 1670 and 1680, the introduction of the cacao tree to the West Indies (Martinique) dramatically lowered the price of cocoa and its chocolate products, making them available to all levels of society.

Preceding pages:
Saxe porcelain pot and Limoges coffee
cup, 19th century.

Pots and Jugs

Prior to the late seventeenth century, a single all-purpose pot was used for tea, coffee, and chocolate. The teapot or coffeepot began to be distinguishable only in the later years of Louis XIV. Originally the teapot was quite small, used only for pouring boiling water over the tea leaves in the cup. It was oval or pear shaped, and pot-bellied. Like the coffeepot, it had a long curving spout, a shapely handle, and a bulging lid with a bump on top.

Shapes

From the moment when tea drinkers began brewing their tea leaves in the teapot itself, it began to grow in stature. Before long a small, sievelike barrier was installed between the base of the spout and the main body of the pot, allowing the tea to be separated from the leaves. The spherical teapot made its first appearance in about 1720. Most antique French teapots were made in towns that maintained close ties with England, such as Lille, Douai, Arras, Valenciennes, Bordeaux, and Paris.

The first coffeepots, dating from the end of the seventeenth century, had flat sides and were called *marabouts* after the Asian kettles of that name. They had a beak set high up in the wall of the pot, allowing the liquid to be poured off the coffee grounds as they settled to the bottom. In the late eighteenth century, coffeepot types ranged from the so-called *egoiste*, which yielded a single cup, to the family pot—mainly manufactured in northern France—which made up to a dozen cups. Between the reigns of Louis XIV and Napoleon III, the shape of the coffeepot altered little; it had a curved outline, three feet, a projecting S-shaped handle made of turned ivory or ebony, and a beaked spout that was sometimes shaped like the neck of a swan. The only substantial variations were in the decorative details, such as rounded corners and straight or crooked sides.

The chocolate jug tended to have the same forms and decorations as the coffeepot: tall, pear shaped, and often with three feet. The only difference was its notched lid, through where the handle of the chocolate whisk was placed. The whisk was made of boxwood, with grooves at the top end so it could be twiddled between the fingers to whip the chocolate and milk to a froth, just as the Indians did.

In the late nineteenth century, serving tea was of great importance. It required plates, flatware, glasses, and platters for the cakes, sweets, fruits, and syrups that accompanied the tea. The tea itself was brewed on a side table, where there might be a samovar or an old French kettle.

It was not until 1925, when the influence of Jean Puiforcat began to spread that the shapes of coffeepots and teapots were completely renewed. They became simpler, squatter, plainer, and less adorned, with beautiful handles made of rare wood.

Sets and Services

The breakfast set (*cabaret* in French) consisted of a tray, a teapot, a coffeepot, a creamer, a sugar bowl, and a single cup and saucer. The word *cabaret* derives from the small table formerly used for serving tea and liqueurs; later it came to mean a tea or coffee service proper, with several matching cups and saucers. Such sets occasionally came accompanied by a

2.

1. Tea and coffee set in the style of Louis XV.

2. Chocolate pots: Louis XVI with fillets and ribbons, Louis XIV with ovolos and traceries, Louis XVI straight-sided, Louis XV with claw feet, and Louis XVI boss-beaded.

1.

1. Illustration by Achille Deveria, circa 1830.

2. Assorted teapots: "falling pearls," pear-shaped with tight ribbing, wooden handled, and gourd-shaped.

3. Tea set with its own porcelain tray, 19th century.

4. Coffee and tea set, bone china and gilded, 1910.

2.

samovar or a heating stand, or even a bowl for used tea leaves or coffee grounds.

Changing Style

The first pouring pots were in the rocaille manner. In the second half of the eighteenth century, they often stood on three feet, and their sides were either ribbed or flat. During the neoclassical period, they took the shapes of urns, drums, or vases. During the Empire and *Directoire* eras, the trend for antiquity made them oval, with spindlier legs and spouts resembling a swan's neck. After 1830, there was a return to the styles of Louis XV and Louis XVI, with ribs and chasing; and later, art nouveau contributed its vegetable motifs, which married very well with the natural curves of the teapot. Art deco revolutionized styles by adopting sober, geometric shapes that were plain and unembellished.

Materials

In the early days, tea, coffee, and chocolate were mainly consumed by the aristocracy, and the first pots were made of silver. Vincennes, Paris, Limoges, and Sèvres porcelain and faience pots quickly followed. In the nineteenth century, sterling silver and silver plate coffeepots were preferred, and they were made by all the

great manufacturers of the time—Grattepin, Tétard, Durand, Veyrat, Odiot, Cardeilha, and Christofle among others. More modest tea and coffee sets were produced in large numbers by all the porcelain and faience makers.

Tisanières or Herbal Tea Sets

The French *tisanière* usually consisted of a pouring pot, a cylinder open at the top and sides, and a cup containing a wick and burning oil for keeping the *tisane*, or herbal tea, warm while creating a faint light.

These utensils were rare in the eighteenth century, largely because herbal teas were regarded as purely medicinal: people only began drinking them for pleasure in the nineteenth century.

During the Empire period, *tisanières* were manufactured in plain white porcelain, occasionally with a decorative border. Later they were decorated with patterns, tableaux, and landscapes.

In the time of Louis XVIII and Charles X, they blossomed into reproductions of famous paintings and military, historical, mythological, and biblical scenes.

The faience *tisanières* of Apt and Lunéville are considered the most beautiful, along with the porcelain models of Paris and Limoges.

1. Full set offered by Christofle in the style of Louis XV. Top to bottom and left to right: creamer, tea bowl, coffeepot, boiler, kettle, tray, sugar bowl, milk jug, and teapot.

2. Fine porcelain coffee pot and coffee cups, Restoration.

3. Sterling silver teapot with wooden handle, circa 1925.

4. English milk jug and teapot for a hotel.

5. Gilded-edged, porcelain sugar bowl, circa 1925.

1.

TIPS FOR COLLECTORS

Coffeepots are much more abundant on the secondhand market than teapots and therefore considerably cheaper. If you are thinking of buying a silver pot, verify that the soldering work around the spout, feet, and handle is in good condition.

Chocolate jugs are rarely used nowadays, but they make attractive decorative items. When purchasing a **tisanière**, make sure that all the components are included in the set.

Antique pieces are twice as valuable if their hallmarks are visible in the correct location. A piece's richness of ornament is an important criterion of value, as are its age, provenance, and the renown of its maker.

Art deco sets are always at a premium, but you can still buy attractive porcelain services for bargain prices.

Pros and cons of resilvering

Resilvering is a costly and time-consuming process that involves numerous manual procedures. It is never wise to think that it will be cheaper to buy and resilver a worn coffeepot than to purchase one in good condition.

Nevertheless resilvering can pay dividends in the case of historically interesting or very precious pieces, or objects with a strong sentimental value.

To keep teapots and coffeepots smelling fresh, drop in a lump of sugar before putting them away.

Don't try to repair leaky spouts or loose handles. Leave these jobs to a specialist.

3.

5.

Cups

The new beverages—tea, coffee, and chocolate—required their own specially made cups. In the early days, tea was taken in the Chinese manner from little porcelain bowls imported by the East India Company. The invention of a cup with a handle—the teacup as we know it today—was attributed to the Meissen porcelain works in the first half of the eighteenth century. The delicacy and lightness of soft-paste porcelain made it an ideal material for teacups, which were painted by the period's greatest masters of porcelain decoration.

Early Forms and Shapes

Tea and coffee started out in Europe as rare and precious substances that only the wealthy could afford. Soft-paste porcelain manufacturers such as Saint-Cloud, Vincennes, Sèvres, Chantilly, and Mennec produced wonderfully delicate, hand-painted cups for them. At first, there was only one form: it had a lid and was used for both beverages.

In the mid-eighteenth century, Saint-Cloud, Vincennes, and Sèvres began making cups in different sizes: the smallest was known as a *mignonnette*, and the most commonly used measured about $2^1/_2$ inches in height. By the end of the century, there was a clear difference between the cups used for the each of the three drinks. Coffee cups had a cylindrical shape with equal diameter and height; the chocolate cup was larger than the coffee cup and had two handles; and the teacup was slightly widemouthed. In 1784, gilded porcelain ceased to be a Sèvres monopoly.

1. Porcelain teacups, gilded-rimmed with serrated pattern. Limoges, 19th century.

2. Porcelain cup and saucer. Manufacture de Sceaux, 18th century.

3. Rocaille two-handled porcelain cup with cover. Custine stamped. Manufacture de Niderviller, 18th century.

4. Hard-paste porcelain teacup and saucer, lobed and boss-beaded. 1880–1890.

5. *Trembleuse* cup and saucer. Sèvres, 1902–1907.

6. Porcelain cup and saucer. Manufacture de Vincennes, 1753.

7. Porcelain "milk cup" with motifs imitated from Asian, Meissen, and Saint-Cloud originals. Manufacture de Vincennes, 18th century.

1.

2.

3.

1. , *Á la reine*, hard-paste porcelain cup with cover. Manufacture du Comte d'Artois, Limoges, 1774–1789.

2. Empire porcelain cup.

3. Hard-paste porcelain cup with serrated pattern and gilded edges. Manufacture Pierre Antoine Hannong, Paris, circa 1775.

4. Porcelain cups with flowerets. Limoges, 19th century.

5. White porcelain "moustache" cup. Limoges, late 19th century.

6. *The Waitress*, oil on canvas by John Robert Dicksee, 1872.

7. English porcelain teacup, plate, and cake dish. Royal Doulton, late 19th century.

Then, the discovery of kaolin led to the founding of a number of bone china potteries, notably in Paris and the Limoges region, which were at last freed to meet the contemporary demand for rich decoration. Alongside such simple patterns as scattered flowers against a white background, they produced cups that were entirely covered with multicolored ornamentation outlined in gold.

During the Empire period, many porcelain manufacturers assigned the decoration of their pieces to *chambrelans*, or specialist painters, who worked at home. After that the porcelain manufacturers of Sèvres began making small masterpieces of lightness and elegance in muslin porcelain, whose immaculate white was ideal for tea since it allowed people to appreciate the tea's delicate color.

Trembleuse and à la reine Cups

The *trembleuse* cup contradicted its name, since it was notably stable, standing square in its high saucer. It was mainly used for drinking chocolate. It usually had handles and occasionally came with a lid of its own. The *à la reine* cup, also called a milk goblet, was used during breakfast and had the shape of a plain truncated cone— a Sèvres invention. Some were made without handles or lids, while others had both.

The cup known as *gobelet Calabre* ("Calabrian goblet") was slightly rounded at its base with an wide mouth. The litron (literally meaning "liquid measure") cup, with or without a lid, was perfectly cylindrical and the direct ancestor of our own coffee cup.

With the Empire period came the jasmine cup, which was used for chocolate. This cup was slightly widemouthed with a stem and stand and was commonly decorated with animal claws. It had two coiled handles that projected above its bowl.

The tiny *tasse canard* ("duck" cup) was used for dipping sugar lumps into a tiny pool of coffee. The filter cup, or herbal tea cup, was much larger and had its own built-in filtering component. Finally, the broth bowl came with a broad mouth, a lid, and two side handles.

TIPS FOR COLLECTORS

If you find a set of cups without matching saucers, don't assume the saucers have all been lost or broken. In the old days, many people preferred to buy sterling silver or silver-plated saucers to go with their cups. Porcelain cups from Paris are still available at highly reasonable prices, which is remarkable given their rarity. If the cup's interior decoration matches that of its exterior or if it is signed by the maker, it will have greater value.

Plenty of common but charming porcelain cups and saucers can be found on the market at reasonable prices. By contrast, genuine eighteenth-century pieces are very expensive.

5.

7.

1.

1. Assorted designs and shapes
for porcelain teacups, from an
English catalogue.

2. Top: faience tableware
from various French potteries,
19th and 20th century.

Bottom: English porcelain from
Minton and French porcelain
from Sarreguemines.

3. Coffee set with flower medallion
decoration, Limoges.

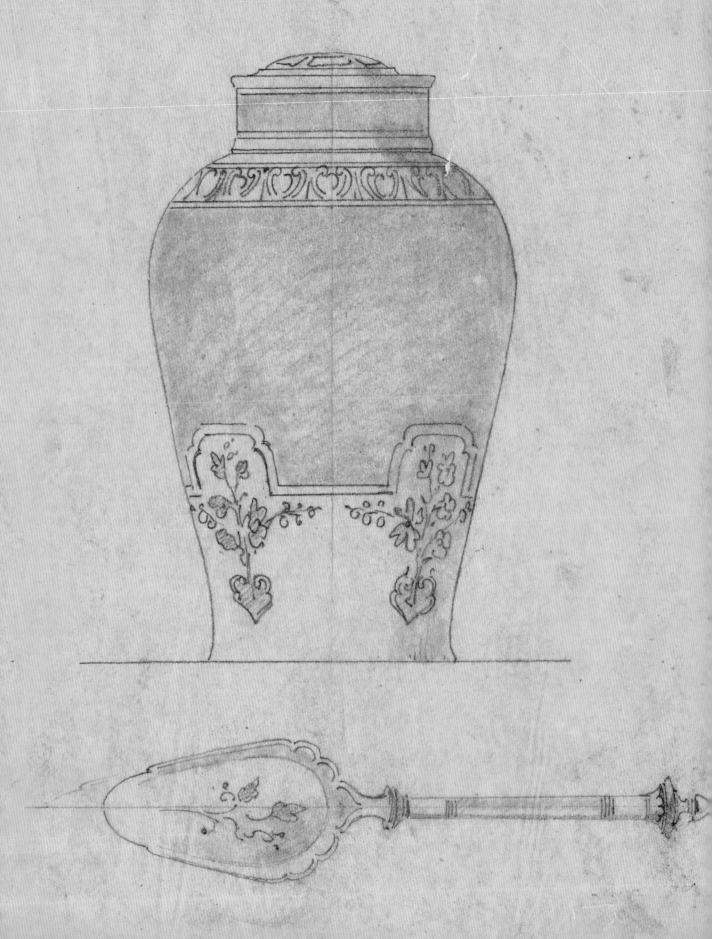

1.

2.

Accessories

Trays, sugar shakers, sugar bowls, tea strainers, and jam dishes are the kinds of accessories whose presence alongside breakfast coffee or tea is in itself a charming refinement.

3.

Matching Trays

From the sophisticated silver tray to its wooden version, by way of wickerwork, marquetry, and painted metal, there is a wide choice—and because few collectors are really interested in trays, there are bargains to be had.

In the eighteenth century, the tray was used to display specific dishes or services; it was made of the same material as the service and had the same outlines. Thus the round trays were used for *pots à oille*, and the oval ones for terrines and porringers—all made of ornate silver or delicate hand-painted porcelain. Similarly, breakfast, tea, and coffee were served on round, square, or triangular trays matching the services, whether they were in ceramic or silverware. Many smaller trays were designed to accompany bowls of ice cream, milk jugs, or creamers. Smallest of all were the ones that came with oil cruets, butter dishes, and sugar bowls.

Serving Trays

In the nineteenth century, the serving tray was essential to the household. It was a simple item, usually made of varnished oak or walnut in the *bistrot* style. It existed in many sizes and was most often used for carrying tea, coffee, or liqueurs. In their grander English form, they were the removable tops of small tables. The end of the century saw the appearance of papier-mâché and metal trays with painted designs against a black background. Foreign influences had their effect, notably those of China, Japan, and the Middle East. Wooden, mother-of-pearl encrusted trays from Syria, as well as lacquered trays and trays made of straw marquetry or rattan, competed with the traditional European ones. But the invention of the electroplating technique made possible the manufacture of magnificent formal trays with beautifully engraved handles, whose decoration recalled the great period of rocaille; these were a major feature of wedding sets.

In the early twentieth century and throughout the art nouveau era, wood was the preferred material for trays—generally pale fruitwood, inlaid with vegetable designs. In the art deco years that ensued, silver trays with grips or handles made of exotic wood or stone gained popularity, as did simple burled wood trays lined with silver.

4.

5.

6.

1. Sugar shakers: matching cap and flat glass sides; single hole cap and glass bottom; oval, grooved sides, and all-metal; Louis XVI, all-metal; and boss-beaded cap and glass bottom.

3. Two 18th-century sterling silver sugar shakers, silver sugar bowl and spoon, and vermeil spoon.

1.

2. Two wooden tea tables, with silver-plated tray tops and complete tea and coffee sets.

2.

Sugar Shakers

Cane sugar in the early days was viewed as a rare and expensive condiment, along with salt and spices. It was kept under lock and key when away from the table and stood alone when it was on it. From the seventeenth century onward, it was more and more widely consumed, in drinks and sauces. The sugar shaker was used between the mid-seventeenth century and the mid-eighteenth century. At first, it was cone-shaped and graduated to the form of a baluster around 1700. It was made in two parts that could be screwed or fitted together, and was filled either from the bottom—which was corked—or from the top. Its removable head was full of tiny holes through which the sugar could be shaken out. It was originally made of silver, but the early faience potteries soon began making sugar shakers using the hot firing process: Nevers with its characteristic cobalt blue, Rouen with its wrought iron and lambrequin motifs, and Moustiers with its Bérain designs.

The slow firing technique later became dominant in this area, including the Chinese patterns of Sincény, and the refined decorations of Saint Jean du Désert, Leroy of Marseille, and Hannong of Strasbourg. The stoneware sugar shakers from Lunéville and Niderviller and the soft-paste porcelain ones made at Chantilly, Saint-Cloud, Vincennes, and Sévres were also very popular, as were the simple glass versions made in Normandy and their taller, more elegant cousins of Tours. Very fine shakers made of opaline and cut crystal were produced by the glassworks of Clichy, Saint-Louis, and Baccarat, before the utensil was rendered obsolete around 1750 by the advent of the sugar bowl and sugar pot.

Sugar Pots and Sugar Bowls

The sugar shaker gave way to the sugar bowl, a kind of small oval basin with four or more sides that had its own tray—either separate or attached to its bottom—and its own porcelain or silver spoon with holes in it for scattering the condiment. Sugar bowls were integral features of the centerpiece or *surtout*; some were boat shaped, with slightly raised ends. The round sugar bowl, on the other hand, was a fixture at the breakfast table.

The invention of a process for extracting sugar from sugar beet, during the Empire period, made sugar far cheaper and more readily available, and the sugar bowl became a widespread, standard item. Yet during this time, sugar also lost its permanent place on the table, only appearing when the dessert was served, inside a transparent crystal shaker with a perforated silver top. Sometimes it was entirely made of sterling silver or silver plate, and recaptured the baluster-shape of the original sugar shakers of the early eighteenth century.

The sugar bowl has kept its place as an indispensable companion to hot drinks and beverages, and it is the formal accessory of any tea or coffee tray worthy of the name. Whether made in sterling silver, silver plate, or porcelain, it is invariably matched with the pot, along with the creamer.

1. Assorted tea strainers with handles.

2. Assorted tea strainers that fit into the spouts of teapots.

3. Candy bowl, silver and crystal, 1920s.

4. 19th-century porcelain sugar bowl on a stand with cornflowers decorations.

5. Crystal sugar shaker with silver top; a restaurant model by Christofle.

6. Small, silver ice cream bowls, 19th century.

Following pages:
Still Life with Salad Greens, Édouard Vuillard, circa 1887–1888.

The Preserve Dish

Just before the French Revolution, the Indian habit of eating jams and preserves at the end of a meal became common in Europe, lasting until the mid-nineteenth century. The great silversmiths Froment-Meurice and Veyrat, among others, created spectacular preserve dishes, which took the form of a crystal basin with a lid, held in a carefully decorated metal frame with a stand. The rim was slotted to receive a dozen little spoons. Later the preserve dish disappeared from the dinner table to resurface on a much-reduced scale at breakfast, becoming a discreet, little covered crystal pot with a silver-plated lid. The lid sometimes had a notch in it for a jam spoon.

The Cookie Jar

This was probably an English invention: a beautifully wrought object made of porcelain or cut or pressed crystal, with a silver mounting, handle, and cover. It was shaped like a small barrel, or was plainly cylindrical, square, or rectangular.

TIPS FOR COLLECTORS

Sugar shakers are rare; Rouen porcelain baluster-shaped shakers are particularly sought after.

By contrast, there are plenty of crystal preserve dishes, which make excellent fruit bowls.

1.   2.

3.

4.

5.

6.

Acknowledgements

Christian Sarramon wishes to express his warm gratitude to the following people, who allowed him access to their collections or otherwise helped with the photographs for this book:

Inès, Béatrice Augié ("Jardin Secrand," Deauville), Ysabel and Pierre Bels, Safia Bendali, Élisabeth Brac de La Perrière, Franck Delmarcelle, Clodine Demoncheaux, Denise and Jean-Marie Derisbourg, Martine de Fontanes ("La Maison d'Uzès," Uzès), Brigitte Forgeur, Christine and Michel Guérard (Eugénie-les-Bains), Dorothée de la Houssaye, Jean-François Le Guillou (Marché Vernaison, Saint-Ouen), Anne-Marie Mesnil ("La Maison de Tara," Boissy-Maugis), Béatrice Pelpel, Chantal and François Perrard, Pascale and Philippe Pierrelée, Nello Renault, Caroline de Roquemaurel, Caroline de Roquette, Jean-Claude Roucheray, and Catherine Synave. Special thanks, also, to L'Argenterie de Turenne (Paris) and la Maison d'Horbé (La Perrière, Orne).

The publishers are particularly grateful to Anne Gros and Magali Lacroix, of the Musée Christofle (Saint-Denis), to the Manufacture de Porcelaine Haviland (Limoges), and to the Musée de Sarreguemines. These institutions placed their archives and photographs at our disposal. Special thanks are also due to Sylvie Gabriel, who kindly gave access to material from the Photothèque Hachette.

Photography Credits

Editorial Director: Odile Perrard
with collaboration of Aurélie Dombes, Florence Renner,
Nathalie Lefebvre, and Clémentine Petit
Art Director: Sabine Houplain
Art Assistant: Laurent Nicole
Design and Layout: Ellen Gögler
Production: Nicole Thiériot-Pichon
English Translation: Anthony Roberts
Color Separation: Reproscan, Italy

First published in the United States of America in 2006 by
Rizzoli International Publications, Inc.
300 Park Avenue South
New York, NY 10010
www.rizzoliusa.com

Originally published in French in 2005 as
La Passion des Arts de la Table by
Èditions du Chêne
A division of Hachette Livres
43 quai de Grenelle
75905 Paris Cedex 15
France

ISBN-10: 0-8478-2844-1
ISBN-13: 978-0-8478-2844-9

Library of Congress Control Number: 2006925128

2006 2007 2008 2009 / 10 9 8 7 6 5 4 3 2 1

Printed in China